HOW TO TEPS

점수대별 TEPS 실전 모의고사

실 전 력
Level 1

How to TEPS 실전력 Level 1

지은이 넥서스 TEPS연구소
펴낸이 안용백
펴낸곳 (주)도서출판 넥서스

출판신고 1992년 4월 3일 제311-2002-2호 ①

121-840 서울시 마포구 서교동 394-2
Tel (02)330-5500 Fax (02)330-5555

ISBN 978-89-5797-417-9 18740

www.nexusEDU.kr
NEXUS Edu는 (주)도서출판 넥서스의 초·중·고 학습물 전문 브랜드입니다.

텝스 입문자를 위한 가장 쉬운 실전 모의고사

HOW TO
TEPS

넥서스 TEPS연구소 지음

점수대별 TEPS 실전 모의고사

실 전 력
Level 1

NEXUS Edu

1999년 1월 첫 TEPS 정기시험 시행 이후 120회를 훌쩍 넘으면서 TEPS는 이제 명실공히 한국인의 영어능력을 가장 객관적이면서 과학적으로 테스팅하는 시험으로 자리매김을 하였습니다.

TEPS 시험 유형을 자세히 분석해 보면 기존의 영어능력 검정시험과 확연히 다른 두 가지 점을 파악할 수 있을 겁니다. 문법과 어휘 영역에서 문어체 표현뿐만 아니라 구어체 표현까지 다양하게 출시된다는 것과 테스팅 타임(2시간 20분) 동안 처리해야 할 문제 정보량이 너무나 방대하기 때문에 TEPS만의 독특한 문제 유형에 익숙해지지 않으면 시간 안에 주어진 문제를 다 풀기가 버겁다는 것입니다. 따라서 TEPS 문제 유형에 익숙해지도록, 소위 말해서 전천후 TEPS 체질로 영어 학습 환경을 완전히 바꾸어야 TEPS 시험에서 고득점을 얻을 수 있습니다.

이러한 문제 유형 파악을 위해 단시간에 가장 효과적인 학습 방법은 시험 출제 경향과 유사한 문제들을 많이 경험하는 것이라는 것을 TEPS를 준비해 본 수험생이라면 누구나 알 것입니다. 시중에 TEPS 모의고사 문제집은 이미 많이 나와 있지만 수험생 각자의 학업 성취 목표에 따라 난이도를 제대로 조절한 모의고사 교재는 아직 없는 것을 발견하고 이번에 넥서스 TEPS연구소 연구원들이 난이도별 모의고사 시리즈를 개발하게 됐습니다.

보다 TEPS 기출문제와 유사한 문제들을 개발하기 위해 연구원들 전원 수시로 TEPS 시험에 응시하며 데이터를 정리했으며, 매력적인 지문과 질문 개발을 위해 미국에 있는 Henry J. Amen IV 외 국내외 여러 박사님들이 끝까지 많은 도움을 주셨습니다. TEPS 입문자들이 쉽게 다가갈 수 있도록 알기 쉬운 풀이와 TEPS의 첫 관문을 넘기 위해 반드시 알아야 할 문제들로만 각 세트를 구성해 이제 〈How to TEPS 실전력 Level 1〉을 출간하게 됐습니다. How to TEPS 실전력 시리즈로 TEPS를 시작하는 독자들에게 새로운 도전과 꿈을 향한 도약의 발판이 될 것입니다. TEPS 이상의 비전 성취를 준비하는 수험생들에게 본책이 유익한 동반자가 될 수 있기를 바랍니다.

넥서스 TEPS연구소 연구원 일동

Contents

Actual **Test 3**

TEPS Q & A

1 / TEPS란?

❶ Test of English Proficiency developed by Seoul National University의 약자로 서울대학교 언어교육원에서 개발하고, TEPS관리위원회에서 주관하는 국가공인 영어시험

❷ 1999년 1월 처음 시행 이후 2010년 11월 현재 128회 실시했으며, 연 16회 실시

❸ 정부기관 및 기업의 직원 채용, 인사고과, 해외 파견 근무자 선발과 더불어 대학과 특목고 입학 및 졸업 자격 요건, 국가고시 및 자격 시험의 영어 대체 시험으로 활용

❹ 100여 명의 국내외 유수 대학의 최고 수준 영어 전문가들이 출제하고, 언어 테스팅 분야의 세계적인 권위자인 Bachman 교수(미국 UCLA)와 Oller 교수(미국 뉴멕시코대)로부터 타당성을 검증받음

❺ 말하기-쓰기 시험인 TEPS Speaking & Writing도 별도로 실시 중이며, 2009년 10월부터 이를 통합한 *i*-TEPS 실시

2 / TEPS 시험 구성

영역	Part별 내용	문항수	시간/배점
청해 Listening Comprehension	Part I : 문장 하나를 듣고 이어질 대화 고르기	15	55분 400점
	Part II : 3문장의 대화를 듣고 이어질 대화 고르기	15	
	Part III : 6~8 문장의 대화를 듣고 질문에 해당하는 답 고르기	15	
	Part IV : 담화문의 내용을 듣고 질문에 해당하는 답 고르기	15	
문법 Grammar	Part I : 대화문의 빈칸에 적절한 표현 고르기	20	25분 100점
	Part II : 문장의 빈칸에 적절한 표현 고르기	20	
	Part III : 대화에서 어법상 틀리거나 어색한 부분 고르기	5	
	Part IV : 단문에서 문법상 틀리거나 어색한 부분 고르기	5	
어휘 Vocabulary	Part I : 대화문의 빈칸에 적절한 단어 고르기	25	15분 100점
	Part II : 단문의 빈칸에 적절한 단어 고르기	25	
독해 Reading Comprehension	Part I : 지문을 읽고 빈칸에 들어갈 내용 고르기	16	45분 400점
	Part II : 지문을 읽고 질문에 가장 적절한 내용 고르기	21	
	Part III : 지문을 읽고 문맥상 어색한 내용 고르기	3	
총계	13개 Parts	200	140분 990점

☆ **IRT** (Item Response Theory)에 의하여 최고점이 990점, 최저점이 10점으로 조정됨.

3 / TEPS 시험 응시 정보

현장 접수
❶ www.teps.or.kr에서 인근 접수처 확인
❷ 준비물: 응시료 33,000원(현금만 가능), 증명사진 1매(3×4 cm)
❸ 접수처 방문: 해당 접수기간 평일 오전 10시 ~ 오후 5시

인터넷 접수
❶ TEPS관리위원회 홈페이지 접속 www.teps.or.kr
❷ 준비물: 스캔한 사진 파일, 응시료 결제를 위한 신용카드 및 은행 계좌
❸ 응시료: 33,000원(일반) / 17,000원(군인) / 36,000원(추가 접수)

4 / TEPS 시험 당일 정보

❶ 고사장 입실 완료: 9시 30분(일요일) / 3시(토요일)
❷ 준비물: 신분증, 컴퓨터용 사인펜, 수정테이프, 수험표, 시계
❸ 유효한 신분증
　성인: 주민등록증, 운전면허증, 여권, 공무원증, 현역간부 신분증, 군무원증, 주민등록증 발급 신청 확인서, 외국인 등록증
　초·중고생: 학생증, 여권, 청소년증, 주민등록증, 주민등록증 발급 신청 확인서, TEPS 신분확인 증명서
❹ 시험 시간: 2시간 20분 (중간에 쉬는 시간 없음, 각 영역별 제한시간 엄수)
❺ 성적 확인: 약 2주 후 인터넷에서 조회 가능

All about the TEPS

Listening Comprehension 60문항

Choose the most appropriate response to the statement. (15문항)

문제유형 질의 응답 문제를 다루며 한 번만 들려주고, 내용은 일상의 구어체 표현으로 구성되어 있다.

> W   I wish my French were as good as yours.
> M   _____

(a) Yes, I'm going to visit France.
✔ (b) Thanks, but I still have a lot to learn.
(c) I hope it works out that way.
(d) You can say that again.

번역 W 당신처럼 프랑스어를 잘하면 좋을 텐데요.
M _____

(a) 네, 프랑스를 방문할 예정이에요.
(b) 고마워요. 하지만 아직도 배울 게 많아요.
(c) 그렇게 잘 되기를 바라요.
(d) 당신 말이 맞아요.

Choose the most appropriate response to complete the conversation. (15문항)

문제유형 두 사람이 A-B-A-B 순으로 대화하는 형식이며, 한 번만 들려준다.

> W   I wish I earned more money.
> M   You could change jobs.
> W   But I love the field I work in.
> M   _____

(a) I think it would be better.
✔ (b) Ask for a raise then.
(c) You should have a choice in it.
(d) I'm not that interested in money.

번역 W 돈을 더 많이 벌면 좋을 텐데요.
M 직장을 바꾸지 그래요?
W 하지만 난 지금 일하고 있는 분야가 좋아요.
M _____

(a) 더 좋아질 거라고 생각해요.
(b) 그러면 급여를 올려 달라고 말해요.
(c) 그 안에서 선택권이 있어야 해요.
(d) 돈에 그렇게 관심이 있지는 않아요.

Choose the option that best answers the question. (15문항)

문제유형   비교적 긴 대화문. 대화문과 질문은 두 번, 선택지는 한 번 들려준다.

M   Hello. You're new here, aren't you?
W   Yes, it's my second week. I'm Karen.
M   What department are you in?
W   Customer service, on the first floor.
M   I see. I'm in sales.
W   So, you'll be working on commission, then.
M   Yes. I like that, but it's very stressful sometimes.

Q: Which is correct according to the conversation?
(a) The man and woman work in the same department.
✔ (b) The woman works in the customer service department.
(c) The man thinks the woman's job is stressful.
(d) The woman likes working for commissions.

번역   M 안녕하세요. 새로 오신 분이시죠?
W 예, 여기 온 지 2주째예요. 전 캐런이에요.
M 어느 부서에서 근무하시나요?
W 1층 고객 지원부에서 일해요.
M 그렇군요. 전 영업부에서 일해요.
W 그러면 커미션제로 일하시는군요.
M 네. 좋기는 하지만 가끔은 스트레스를 많이 받아요.

Q: 대화에 따르면 옳은 것은?
(a) 남자와 여자는 같은 부서에서 일한다.
(b) 여자는 고객 지원부에서 일한다.
(c) 남자는 여자의 일이 스트레스가 많다고 생각한다.
(d) 여자는 커미션제로 일하는 것을 좋아한다.

All about the TEPS

 Choose the option that best answers the question. (15문항)

문제유형   담화문의 주제, 세부 사항, 사실 여부 및 이를 근거로 한 추론 등을 다룬다.

> Confucian tradition placed an emphasis on the values of the group over the individual. It also taught that workers should not question authority. This helped industrialization by creating a pliant populace willing to accept long hours and low wages and not question government policies. The lack of dissent helped to produce stable government and this was crucial for investment and industrialization in East Asian countries.

Q: What can be inferred from the lecture?
(a) Confucianism promoted higher education in East Asia.
(b) East Asian people accept poverty as a Confucian virtue.
✔ (c) Confucianism fostered industrialization in East Asia.
(d) East Asian countries are used to authoritarian rule.

번역   유교 전통은 개인보다 조직의 가치를 강조했습니다. 또한 노동자들에게 권위에 대해 의문을 제기하지 말라고 가르쳤습니다. 이것은 장시간 노동과 저임금을 기꺼이 감수하고 정부의 정책에 의문을 제기하지 않는 고분고분한 민중을 만들어 냄으로써 산업화에 도움이 되었습니다. 반대의 부재는 안정적인 정부를 만드는 데 도움이 되었고, 이는 동아시아 국가들에서 투자와 산업화에 결정적이었습니다.

Q: 강의로부터 유추할 수 있는 것은?
(a) 유교는 동아시아에서 고등교육을 장려했다.
(b) 동아시아 사람들은 유교의 미덕으로 가난을 받아들인다.
(c) 유교는 동아시아에서 산업화를 촉진했다.
(d) 동아시아 국가들은 독재주의 법칙에 익숙하다.

Grammar 50문항

PART I

Choose the best answer for the blank. (20문항)

문제유형 A, B 두 사람의 짧은 대화 중에 빈칸이 있다. 동사의 시제 및 수 일치, 문장의 어순 등이 주로 출제되며, 구어체 문법의 독특한 표현들을 숙지하고 있어야 한다.

> A   Should I just keep waiting _____ me back?
> B   Well, just waiting doesn't get anything done, does it?

    (a) for the editor write
✔ (b) until the editor writes
    (c) till the editor writing
    (d) that the editor writes

번역 A   편집자가 나한테 답장을 쓸 때까지 기다리고만 있어야 합니까?
       B   글쎄요, 단지 기다리고 있다고 해서 무슨 일이 이루어지는 건 아니겠죠?

PART II

Choose the best answer for the blank. (20문항)

문제유형 문어체 문장을 읽고 어법상 빈칸에 적절한 표현을 고르는 유형으로 세부적인 문법 자체에 대한 이해는 물론 구문에 대한 이해력도 테스트한다.

> All passengers should remain seated at _____ times.

    (a) any
    (b) some
✔ (c) all
    (d) each

번역 모든 승객들은 항상 앉아 있어야 합니다.

All about the TEPS

PART III

Identify the option that contains an awkward expression or an error in grammar. (5문항)

문제유형 대화문에서 어법상 틀리거나 어색한 부분이 있는 문장을 고르는 문제로 구성되어 있다.

> (a)　A Where did you go on your honeymoon?
> (b)　B We flew to Bali, Indonesia.
> ✔ (c)　A Did you have good time?
> (d)　B Sure. It was a lot of fun.

번역
(a)　A 신혼여행은 어디로 가셨나요?
(b)　B 인도네시아 발리로 갔어요.
(c)　A 좋은 시간 보내셨어요?
(d)　B 물론이죠. 정말 재미있었어요.

PART IV

Identify the option that contains an awkward expression or an error in grammar. (5문항)

문제유형 한 문단 속에 문법적으로 틀리거나 어색한 문장을 고르는 유형이다.

> (a) Morality is not the only reason for putting human rights on the West's foreign policy agenda. (b) Self-interest also plays a part in the process. (c) Political freedom tends to go hand in hand with economic freedom, which in turn tends to bring international trade and prosperity. (d) A world in which more countries respect basic human rights would be more peaceful place.

번역
(a) 서양의 외교정책 의제에 인권을 상정하는 유일한 이유가 도덕성은 아니다. (b) 자국의 이익 또한 그 과정에 일정 부분 관여한다. (c) 정치적 자유는 경제적 자유와 나란히 나아가는 경향이 있는데, 경제적 자유는 국제 무역과 번영을 가져오는 경향이 있다. (d) 더 많은 국가들이 기본적인 인권을 존중하는 세상은 더 평화로운 곳이 될 것이다.

Vocabulary 50문항

Choose the best answer for the blank. (25문항)

문제유형 A, B 대화 빈칸에 가장 적절한 단어를 넣는 유형이다. 단어의 단편적인 의미보다는 문맥에서 어떻게 쓰였는지 아는 것이 중요하다.

> A   Let's take a coffee break.
> B   I wish I could, but I'm _____ in work.

✔ (a) up to my eyeballs
(b) green around the gills
(c) against the grain
(d) keeping my chin up

번역 A 잠깐 휴식 시간을 가집시다.
B 그러면 좋겠는데 일 때문에 꼼짝도 할 수가 없네요.

(a) ~에 몰두하여
(b) 안색이 나빠 보이는
(c) 뜻이 맞지 않는
(d) 기운 내는

Choose the best answer for the blank. (25문항)

문제유형 문어체 문장의 빈칸에 가장 적절한 단어를 고르는 유형이다. 고난도 어휘의 독특한 용례를 따로 학습해 두어야 고득점이 가능하다.

> It takes a year for the earth to make one _____ around the sun.

(a) conversion
(b) circulation
(c) restoration
✔ (d) revolution

번역 지구가 태양 주위를 한 번 공전하는 데 일 년이 걸린다.
(a) 전환
(b) 순환
(c) 복구
(d) 공전

All about the TEPS

Reading Comprehension 40문항

Choose the option that best completes the passage. (16문항)

문제유형 지문의 논리적인 흐름을 파악하여 문맥상 빈칸에 가장 적절한 선택지를 고르는 문제이다.

> This product is a VCR-sized box that sits on or near a television and automatically records and stores television shows, sporting events and other TV programs, making them available for viewing later. This product lets users watch their favorite program _____. It's TV-on-demand that actually works, and no monthly fees.

　✔ (a) whenever they want to
　(b) wherever they watch TV
　(c) whenever they are on TV
　(d) when the TV set is out of order

번역 이 제품은 텔레비전 옆에 놓인 VCR 크기의 상자로 TV 쇼, 스포츠 이벤트 및 다른 TV 프로그램을 자동으로 녹화 저장하여 나중에 볼 수 있게 해준다. 이 제품은 사용자가 자신이 가장 좋아하는 프로그램을 원하는 시간 언제나 볼 수 있게 해준다. 이것은 실제로 작동하는 주문형 TV로 매달 내는 시청료도 없다.

　(a) 원하는 시간 언제나
　(b) TV를 보는 곳 어디든지
　(c) TV에 나오는 언제나
　(d) TV가 작동되지 않을 때

Choose the option that best answers the question. (21문항)

문제유형 지문에 대한 이해를 측정하는 유형으로 주제 파악, 세부 내용 파악, 논리적 추론을 묻는 문제로 구성되어 있다.

> The pace of bank mergers is likely to accelerate. Recently Westbank has gained far more profit than it has lost through mergers, earning a record of $2.11 billion in 2003. Its shareholders have enjoyed an average gain of 28% a year over the past decade, beating the 18% annual return for the benchmark S&P stock index. However, when big banks get bigger, they have little interest in competing for those basic services many households prize. Consumers have to pay an average of 15% more a year, or $27.95, to maintain a regular checking account at a large bank instead of a smaller one.

　Q: What is the main topic of the passage?
　(a) Reasons for bank mergers
　✔ (b) Effects of bank mergers
　(c) The merits of big banks
　(d) Increased profits of merged banks

번역　은행 합병 속도가 가속화될 전망이다. 최근 웨스트 뱅크가 2003년 21억 1천만 달러의 수익을 기록함으로써 합병으로 잃은 것보다 훨씬 더 많은 수익을 얻었다. 웨스트 뱅크 주주들은 지난 10년간 S&P 지수의 연간 수익률 18%를 웃도는 연평균 수익률 28%를 누려왔다. 하지만 규모가 더욱 커진 대형 은행들은 많은 가구가 중요하게 생각하는 기본 서비스에 대한 경쟁에는 별 관심을 두고 있지 않다. 소비자들은 작은 은행 대신 대형 은행의 보통 당좌예금 계정을 유지하기 위해 연평균 15% 이상, 즉 27달러 95센트를 지불해야 한다.

Q: 지문의 소재는?
(a) 은행 합병의 이유
(b) 은행 합병의 영향
(c) 대형 은행의 장점
(d) 합병된 은행들의 수익 증가

Identify the option that does NOT belong. (3문항)

문제유형　한 문단에서 전체의 흐름상 어색한 내용을 고르는 유형이다.

> Communication with language is carried out through two basic human activities: speaking and listening. (a) These are of particular importance to psychologists, for they are mental activities that hold clues to the very nature of the human mind. (b) In speaking, people put ideas into words, talking about perceptions, feelings, and intentions they want other people to grasp. (c) In listening, people decode the sounds of words they hear to gain the intended meaning. (d) Language has stood at the center of human affairs throughout human history.

번역　언어로 이루어지는 의사소통은 두 가지 기본적인 인간 활동인 말하기와 듣기에 의해 수행된다. (a) 이 두 가지는 심리학자들에게 각별한 중요성을 지니는데, 이는 두 가지가 인간의 심성 본질 자체에 대한 단서를 쥐고 있는 정신적 활동이기 때문이다. (b) 말할 때 사람들은 다른 사람들이 이해하기를 원하는 지각과 감정, 의도 등을 말하면서 아이디어들을 단어로 표현한다. (c) 들을 때 사람들은 의도된 뜻을 간파하기 위해 들리는 단어의 소리를 해독한다. (d) 언어는 인류의 역사를 통틀어 인간 활동의 중심에 있어 왔다.

Actual Test 1

LISTENING
COMPREHENSION

Part I **Questions 1—15**

You will now hear fifteen conversation fragments, each made up of a single spoken statement followed by four spoken responses. Choose the most appropriate response to the statement.

Part II **Questions 16—30**

You will now hear fifteen conversation fragments, each made up of three spoken statements followed by four spoken responses. Choose the most appropriate response to complete the conversation.

Part III   **Questions 31—45**

You will now hear fifteen complete conversations. For each item, you will hear a conversation and its corresponding question, both of which will be read twice. Then you will hear four options which will be read only once. Choose the option that best answers the question.

Part IV   **Questions 46—60**

You will now hear fifteen spoken monologues. For each item, you will hear a monologue and its corresponding question, both of which will be read twice. Then you will hear four options which will be read only once. Choose the option that best answers the question.

GRAMMAR

DIRECTIONS

This part of the exam tests your grammar skills. You will have 25 minutes to complete the 50 questions. Be sure to follow the directions given by the proctor.

Part I Questions 1—20

Choose the best answer for the blank.

1. A: The printer's broken. Will you fix it?
    B: I wish I _____, but I don't know how.

    (a) can
    (b) could
    (c) would
    (d) should

2. A: Why won't you listen to me?
    B: I'm trying _____ the TV.

    (a) watch
    (b) to watch
    (c) watching
    (d) to watching

3. A: You should send out a lot of college applications.
    B: Well, I _____ that.

    (a) does
    (b) done
    (c) doing
    (d) have done

4. A: I thought we had some bread left.
    B: We _____ it all.

    (a) eat
    (b) are eating
    (c) had been eating
    (d) must have eaten

5. A: Where did you leave my bike?
    B: It's over there _____ the wall.

    (a) for
    (b) onto
    (c) among
    (d) against

6. A: I want to see that new action movie.
    B: Unfortunately, it's not _____ good.

    (a) that
    (b) such
    (c) every
    (d) indeed

7. A: Let's go and see Sarah.
    B: No, she's the one _____ told on me.

    (a) who
    (b) what
    (c) whom
    (d) whose

8. A: What are you so happy about?
    B: _____ I didn't study, I passed the exam.

    (a) Till
    (b) Unless
    (c) Rather than
    (d) Even though

9. A: I'm gaining a lot of weight.
   B: You should avoid _____ sweets and junk food.

   (a) to eat
   (b) eating
   (c) of eating
   (d) to have eaten

10. A: Your nose looks sore. What happened?
    B: _____ around a corner, I bumped into a post.

    (a) Ran
    (b) I ran
    (c) Running
    (d) Was running

11. A: Come and watch TV.
    B: First I have to tidy up _____.

    (a) kitchen
    (b) a kitchen
    (c) the kitchen
    (d) some kitchen

12. A: Which of these two books do you like better?
    B: Neither of them _____ any good.

    (a) is
    (b) be
    (c) are
    (d) were

13. A: I had no money all last week.
    B: _____ that, I would have helped.

    (a) I knew
    (b) Did I know
    (c) That I knew
    (d) Had I known

14. A: Are you sure you don't need help?
    B: Don't worry, I _____.

    (a) am it able to handle
    (b) will handle about it
    (c) can be it able to handle
    (d) will be able to handle it

15. A: When will the customer get the order?
    B: It will be delivered tomorrow to _____.

    (a) he
    (b) his
    (c) him
    (d) theirs

16. A: Are you going to do anything for your vacation?
    B: Yes, I _____ to visit Hawaii for two weeks.

    (a) was planned
    (b) am planning
    (c) have been planned
    (d) will have been planning

17. A: How come you can draw so well?

    B: Well, I have taken _____ lessons.

    (a) few
    (b) little
    (c) a few
    (d) a little

18. A: How did you know Jason took my bike?

    B: I heard him _____ about it to his friend.

    (a) talks
    (b) talked
    (c) talking
    (d) to talk

19. A: Do I really have to go swimming?

    B: It's only if you _____.

    (a) want to
    (b) want to it
    (c) want to that
    (d) want to go it

20. A: Is there a reason you're so late?

    B: _____ on the way here.

    (a) Broke down my car
    (b) My car broke down
    (c) It broke down my car
    (d) Car of mine broke down

Part II **Questions 21—40**

Choose the best answer for the blank.

---

21. The movie director said he wanted to use some new unknown actors _____ in the future.

    (a) in his making movies
    (b) made in movies of his
    (c) in the movies he makes
    (d) for movies making by him

22. _____ societies where political freedom is limited, many people turn to the Internet to voice their opinions.

    (a) By
    (b) As
    (c) In
    (d) On

23. _____ the boy forget his pencils, but he forgot to bring one of his books to school as well.

    (a) Didn't only
    (b) Had not only
    (c) Not only did
    (d) It was not only

24. Betty wondered who the person was _____ to her boyfriend.

    (a) to speak
    (b) had spoken
    (c) speaking
    (d) being spoken

25. The boy was hungry and asked if he could have _____.

    (a) more the rice
    (b) some more rice
    (c) any more of rice
    (d) rice a little more

26. The professor's explanation of the chemistry problem made the students more _____.

    (a) confuse
    (b) confused
    (c) confusing
    (d) to confuse

27. _____ stepped off the bus than it started to rain.

    (a) As soon the old lady
    (b) Sooner had old lady that
    (c) No sooner had the old lady
    (d) Had not the old lady sooner

28. _____ in the wine industry since graduation, the woman considered herself an expert in the field.

    (a) She worked
    (b) To have worked
    (c) Had been working
    (d) Having been working

29. Everyone knows that the clearing of rain forests is bad, _____ countries continue to do it.

    (a) so
    (b) as
    (c) yet
    (d) since

30. Police found explosives in the car _____ the suspected terrorists were traveling.

    (a) that
    (b) where
    (c) of whom
    (d) in which

31. The director promised to make improvements in his department but after a month _____ had changed.

    (a) few
    (b) less
    (c) fewer
    (d) little

32. _____ really compares with the brilliance, learning, and vision of Henry Beston.

    (a) No writer of his time
    (b) His time had no writer
    (c) Not in his time any writer
    (d) Any writer of his time not

33. The couple sat quietly, _____ for the doctor to bring them the results of the blood test.

    (a) wait
    (b) waited
    (c) waiting
    (d) they wait

34. All students _____ to follow the school dress code by their teachers.

    (a) expect
    (b) expecting
    (c) are expected
    (d) must be expecting

35. The worker told his boss that he _____ the report by the time everyone goes out for their lunch break.

(a) finishes
(b) has finished
(c) had been finished
(d) will have finished

36. Sarah could not drink coffee without having two spoons of _____ in it.

(a) sugar
(b) sugars
(c) a sugar
(d) the sugars

37. The police _____ that the man they arrested was not guilty after they had found new evidence.

(a) decide
(b) decided
(c) were decided
(d) had been decided

38. It is really important that the road _____ repaired as soon as possible.

(a) be
(b) has
(c) should
(d) had been

39. Mark got stuck in a traffic jam and that caused him _____ at work late.

(a) arrives
(b) arriving
(c) to arrive
(d) for arriving

40. Thanks to a World Health Organization campaign, smallpox became _____ removed from the world.

(a) major first disease be
(b) the major disease first one
(c) disease to be first major one
(d) the first major disease to be

Part III **Questions 41—45**

Identify the option that contains an awkward expression or an error in grammar.

41. (a) A: Hey, have you seen the car keys anywhere?
    (b) B: The last time I see them was on the kitchen table.
    (c) A: I've already looked there but they weren't there.
    (d) B: Then maybe you should check in the bedroom.

42. (a) A: Brian is complaining about his workload again.
    (b) B: Is he really more work than everyone else is getting?
    (c) A: I'm not sure. We all have different jobs to do.
    (d) B: Well, it's something the team leader should check.

43. (a) A: Look at the sky. I'm guessing it will rain today.
    (b) B: There was nothing about rain on last night's news.
    (c) A: Yeah, but often weather reports on TV is wrong.
    (d) B: That's true. They got it wrong one day last week.

44. (a) A: I heard Janine sent you an email from Paris.
    (b) B: Oh, yeah. She said she doesn't want to return home.
    (c) A: If that's what she said, she can be loving it there.
    (d) B: Well, I can understand why. Paris is a great city.

45. (a) A: Hey, look at this. I matched four numbers in the lotto.
    (b) B: Wow! That was lucky. How much will you get?
    (c) A: I won't find out until I hand in the ticket.
    (d) B: It might be hundred dollars or more. I hope so, anyway.

Part IV   Questions 46—50

Identify the option that contains an awkward expression or an error in grammar.

46. (a) Racing car games are great fun in the arcade because they have seats like a real car. (b) You can feel like you are in a real car as you play the racing game. (c) Now, if you want this same experience at home, it is possible to buy a special simulator seat. (d) It is great for gaming, if only the big problem is that it will cost you over $300.

47. (a) If you are planning to buy a new car, you have to know your financial limit. (b) You have to consider your income, the costs of running a car, maintenance, and car loan repayments. (c) The total cost of owning a car should not be more than ten percent of your total earnings. (d) Once you had worked out these costs, it will help you work out what car you can afford.

48. (a) Miles Franklin's *My Brilliant Career* deserves all the praise it has received for over a century. (b) It is a novel full of free thought and was ahead of its time when publishing in 1901. (c) The novel is about a woman who is strong and independent but who feels trapped by society. (d) She dares to be different, even though she knows she will get in trouble for her actions.

49. (a) For decades people have said that textbooks would be replaced in education. (b) At first they thought television and teaching machines would teach kids instead of books. (c) Then they thought computers would create a teaching revolution where textbooks would not need. (d) But each time new media are introduced, they never take over the special place of textbooks in education.

50. (a) When you get a new puppy, you have to find a name for him or her. (b) If you get stuck, you can name your puppy of a historical person, a hero, or a fictional character. (c) Then you have to teach your puppy the name so he or she comes running when you call. (d) The best way is to say the name every time you talk to your puppy till he or she learns it.

This is the end of the Grammar section. Do NOT move on to the next section until instructed to do so. You are NOT allowed to turn to any other section of the test.

VOCABULARY

Part I **Questions 1—25**

Choose the best answer for the blank.

1. A: You are looking very fit.
   B: Well, I do a lot of _____.

   (a) range
   (b) chance
   (c) volume
   (d) exercise

2. A: Hi, Anne. Good to see you.
   B: Oh, I didn't think I would
   _____ you here.

   (a) add
   (b) note
   (c) meet
   (d) watch

3. A: I find the math we're learning
   quite simple.
   B: Not me. I think it's _____.

   (a) dear
   (b) complicated
   (c) loose
   (d) knotted

4. A: Shall we go out tonight?
   B: No, I'm going to _____ it
   easy tonight.

   (a) fix
   (b) use
   (c) take
   (d) spare

5. A: Will we stay at a hotel downtown?
   B: Yes, I've already _____ our
   room.

   (a) stated
   (b) booked
   (c) formed
   (d) directed

6. A: Why are you crying, Susan?
   B: That boy over there _____
   me.

   (a) hit
   (b) fell
   (c) paid
   (d) stayed

7. A: Hello, where is the toilet, please?
   B: It's just down the _____.

   (a) slip
   (b) roof
   (c) stairs
   (d) shelf

8. A: I've got nothing good to wear.
   B: You need to buy more _____.

   (a) pieces
   (b) topping
   (c) fashion
   (d) clothing

9. A: It's really raining hard now.
   B: I think we might get _____.

   (a) wet
   (b) stung
   (c) bathed
   (d) watered

10. A: Did you like my gift to you?
    B: Yes, it was a nice _____.

    (a) period
    (b) season
    (c) practice
    (d) surprise

11. A: Why was the dinner cancelled?
    B: Well, not many people could
       _____.

    (a) hire
    (b) bare
    (c) attend
    (d) satisfy

12. A: One of our bathroom taps is
       continuously leaking.
    B: Then, I think we'd better
       _____ a plumber.

    (a) display
    (b) resume
    (c) notice
    (d) contact

13. A: Is our flight really delayed?
    B: Yes, we won't _____ for
       another hour.

    (a) load
    (b) deter
    (c) board
    (d) deplane

14. A: Here's a good place for
       rollerblading.
    B: Right. It's nice and _____.

    (a) flat
    (b) united
    (c) tender
    (d) shallow

15. A: What did the boss want to see you
       about?
    B: He _____ me more work.

    (a) lined
    (b) fitted
    (c) handed
    (d) sorted

16. A: Sally's face is pale and she looks
       really ill.
    B: Yes, I noticed that, too. She's
       definitely _____.

    (a) dull
    (b) unwell
    (c) calm
    (d) harsh

17. A: I like this kind of music.
    B: Not me. I'm not a _____ of
       it.

    (a) fan
    (b) pal
    (c) partner
    (d) support

18. A: How do you like this drawing I
       did?
    B: It's really good. You've got
       _____.

    (a) point
    (b) talent
    (c) measure
    (d) ceremony

19. A: I hope that guy doesn't win the election.

B: Me, too. I won't be _____ for him.

(a) voting
(b) polling
(c) electing
(d) applying

20. A: Oh! What was that loud noise?

B: Sorry. My book _____ the table.

(a) fell off
(b) went out
(c) threw off
(d) came down

21. A: Will you say sorry for what you did?

B: OK, it was my mistake, so I _____.

(a) blame
(b) excuse
(c) sadden
(d) apologize

22. A: Congratulations on your promotion!

B: Thanks. For a while there I was _____ I wouldn't get it.

(a) stable
(b) worried
(c) alert
(d) ideal

23. A: Do you like my new dress? I bought it yesterday.

B: Oh, yes. If you want my opinion, it really _____ you.

(a) models
(b) suits
(c) relates
(d) tightens

24. A: I didn't get much sleep last night.

B: I can tell. You look really _____.

(a) sore
(b) weary
(c) dumb
(d) unclear

25. A: This TV show's boring, don't you think?

B: Yes, turn to something more _____.

(a) filling
(b) creating
(c) releasing
(d) exciting

Part II Questions 26—50

Choose the best answer for the blank.

26. A person can be healthy and free from many diseases if he or she leads a(n) _____ life.

   (a) soft
   (b) ripe
   (c) active
   (d) guilty

27. Some _____ ingredients in Italian cooking are olive oil, cheese, tomatoes, and pasta.

   (a) tight
   (b) basic
   (c) round
   (d) stiff

28. Tennis star Richard Farrell claimed _____ with a win over Giovanni Greco in the first round of the French Open.

   (a) top
   (b) status
   (c) victory
   (d) beating

29. The mortgage _____ has been a problem for a couple of years and is holding up economic recovery.

   (a) tap
   (b) goal
   (c) crisis
   (d) stain

30. An investigation into herbal supplements found that they _____ small amounts of lead and other contaminants.

   (a) drew
   (b) sunk
   (c) tripped
   (d) contained

31. There are plans to _____ a new museum next year in Manhattan's old meatpacking district.

   (a) lay
   (b) rack
   (c) erect
   (d) ground

32. The Internet has useful information, but you can save more money when traveling by getting _____ from actual people.

   (a) risks
   (b) senses
   (c) reuses
   (d) opinions

33. If you want a new laptop and want to get the best _____, then check out our online store.

   (a) rip
   (b) deal
   (c) cost
   (d) trait

34. Unfortunately, in many countries around the world children are still becoming _____ of child slavery.

    (a) bets
    (b) debts
    (c) chains
    (d) victims

35. Riding a horse takes _____ and practice and is not as simple as people think.

    (a) grip
    (b) skill
    (c) trial
    (d) return

36. The woman found it peaceful and _____ to go for a walk in the park.

    (a) airing
    (b) dimming
    (c) floating
    (d) relaxing

37. *The Dragon Chronicles* is such a good novel that it is sure to be _____ into a movie one day.

    (a) famed
    (b) turned
    (c) hinted
    (d) stepped

38. The new printer has a higher resolution so it prints _____ and clearer images than other printers.

    (a) meaner
    (b) sharper
    (c) briefer
    (d) thinner

39. Researchers have _____ that some birds fly over seven thousand miles nonstop when they migrate.

    (a) ordered
    (b) mounted
    (c) relieved
    (d) discovered

40. Five American tourists taken hostage were _____ by their kidnappers on Tuesday and are now safe.

    (a) torn
    (b) retired
    (c) spilled
    (d) released

41. During the colonization of the New World, many tons of gold and silver were _____ back to Spain.

    (a) split
    (b) formed
    (c) herded
    (d) shipped

42. Photographers use a variety of lenses and filters to _____ the photographs they want.

    (a) obtain
    (b) hike
    (c) strike
    (d) pinch

43. The man was _____ because his neighbor was making too much noise.

    (a) fired
    (b) upset
    (c) tracked
    (d) ordinary

44. The latest _____ in skin care is using products that contain gold, but medical experts say gold does not really do anything.

(a) cast
(b) force
(c) trend
(d) streak

45. Women with similar education, skills, and experience as men deserve to receive _____ pay.

(a) exact
(b) noble
(c) equal
(d) proud

46. Patrons are reminded that smoking is not _____ in public areas.

(a) lit
(b) picked
(c) rested
(d) allowed

47. Many people in Britain now believe that the _____ of climate change is not really true.

(a) focus
(b) threat
(c) stroke
(d) balance

48. The quality of the plastic surgeon you choose will determine the _____ of your surgery.

(a) bits
(b) lines
(c) results
(d) fusions

49. During Japan's Jomon Period (13,000 BC to 300 BC), people who _____ the Japanese islands lived by gathering, fishing, and hunting.

(a) landed
(b) inhabited
(c) exited
(d) fulfilled

50. Few novels have achieved both the mass _____ and the literary fame of *To Kill a Mockingbird*.

(a) rate
(b) scheme
(c) attitude
(d) appeal

This is the end of the Vocabulary section. Do NOT move on to the Reading Comprehension section until instructed to do so. You are NOT allowed to turn to any other section of the test.

READING
COMPREHENSION

Part I **Questions 1—16**

Read the passage. Then choose the option that best completes the passage.

---

1. When you need a gift for an anniversary or Valentine's Day, consider
    _____. These can include items such as chocolates,
    cheeses, chocolate-covered fruits, and wine. They are usually made of several
    smaller themed gifts in a basket or another type of container. Often you can choose
    what you like. During occasions such as Valentine's Day, retailers offer seasonal gift
    baskets online or in their stores, so there is a lot of choice.

    (a) sending a romantic gift basket
    (b) giving a voucher instead of flowers
    (c) going online to do all of your shopping
    (d) buying your partner a nice box of chocolates

2. As the population ages, more elderly people will be using home monitoring devices.
    If an elderly person is in trouble, he or she can simply push a button they carry with
    them that is connected to the monitoring device, which automatically contacts a
    central station to say the person has a problem. Operators at the station can then call
    for help and tell relatives that something is wrong. These devices are great around
    the home for _____. Future devices will have GPS
    tracking and will work outside of the home.

    (a) making a loud alarm noise
    (b) controlling home appliances
    (c) helping old people in emergencies
    (d) preventing accidents with medication

3. Summer this year could be worse than last year for the millions of students that
    want summer jobs. State and local governments, who are traditionally among the
    biggest summertime employers, have financial problems and are cutting jobs.
    Money for job programs is also running out. Private companies are also not hiring
    as many students and are waiting for the economy to recover. With so many people
    competing for fewer jobs, students are missing out. For many of them, it will be
    _____.

    (a) the best time of their lives
    (b) a summer without work or money
    (c) the last job before they graduate
    (d) a difficult summer working in the heat

4. Researchers studying termites have found that wherever there were a lot of green circular vegetation patches, termites were living under them. These circular green patches had plants and trees that were greener, bigger, and better than plants and trees in other areas. This was because the termites underneath were loosening the soil and increasing nitrogen levels. The green areas also attract more animals. So termites _____. It is quite a contrast to how people usually see them as pests.

(a) can destroy the vegetation
(b) do a lot of harm to animals
(c) are useful for helping the environment
(d) have more complicated lives than ants

5. If you ever wondered just how bad it is for the soldiers fighting over in Afghanistan, the new book by journalist Ralph Alexander can tell you. It details the stark and frightening reality of what life is truly like on the frontline of the war. Alexander spent 5 months with a group of soldiers, essentially as one of them, except he did not carry a gun—he carried a pen and a camera. He brilliantly captures the emotion and atmosphere of everything going on around him. In this book, you will get

_____.

(a) the truth about Ralph Alexander
(b) a realistic portrayal of the war
(c) the meaning of democratic freedom
(d) a good idea about life with Afghans

6. California's coast has surfing, tourism, and ocean views, and it will soon provide the benefit of _____. Up to a fifth of the state's energy needs could be obtained in this way. California utility Pacific Electric has plans to begin a wave energy project that will generate 100 megawatts of electricity from waves. It will put devices under water that would convert wave energy into electricity, and a cable would then carry the electricity to shore, where it would go into the electrical grid.

(a) energy through using wave power
(b) electricity from the wind
(c) artificial wave generation
(d) cheaper solar energy production

7.

> Dear Editor,
>
> I applaud Alice Blake's article, "End the Welfare State," of June 2. The mindset of many people in this country is to take whatever they can from the State. Hopefully, now that the election is over, the new government will address this issue. People have to start paying their way. The health and education systems would run better if users paid even a small amount for the services they get. Free benefits have ruined our public services. People need to learn responsibility and
>
> _____.
>
> Sincerely,
> Donald Fibster

(a) give to the poor in society
(b) start paying for our services
(c) stop complaining about welfare
(d) vote correctly for a better government

8. Legend has it that the city of Rome was founded by a man named Romulus. It is said that Rome began when he constructed a wall around his village. But it is not known whether Romulus actually existed. Most historians have a different view of how Rome began. They say it started as a number of small villages that had formed around seven hills. As these villages grew, they merged to form one large city. Then, around 750 BC, the leaders of the villages met and decided to

_____.

(a) vote Romulus as Rome's leader
(b) join with the citizens of Rome
(c) build walls around their villages
(d) unite all villages as a Roman city

9. Critics say the full-sized Primo 8X42 binoculars are an excellent choice for most users. Its optics are nearly as good as those of luxury binoculars, so it is good value for the money. The Primo can be used for most purposes and in most situations. It is even designed to be comfortable for eyeglass wearers. Also, you can take them anywhere because they are waterproof and fog-proof. Most reviews say the Primo

_____.

(a) is the best luxury brand available
(b) represents quite a good all-round buy
(c) lacks the quality of expensive binoculars
(d) unfortunately falls short in several areas

10. According to new research, the population of European birds known as blackcaps has been _____. In less than 30 generations of breeding, what was once a single bird group is now two different groups. They have become two species, even though they live together in the same forests. The research found that this was caused by human activities. That means that humans are not only influencing the fate of endangered species, but the fate of common ones as well.

(a) split into two separate and distinct species
(b) put in serious danger of becoming extinct
(c) growing steadily for several generations
(d) forced to relocate because of humans

11. The day started cold and clear today, with an overnight low of 6.3 degrees C, but a cold front is coming in and we are likely to get heavy showers tonight. There is also a risk of a thunderstorm, along with strong north to north-westerly winds. Similar weather is expected tomorrow morning. In the afternoon, however, you can expect the opposite, with _____. Conditions should remain fine for the weekend.

(a) hail and snowstorms
(b) fine and sunny weather
(d) showers and windy weather
(c) conditions becoming much cooler

12. Originally, workmen's clothes were made out of denim and only workmen wore denim. Then Levi Strauss made the first blue jeans out of denim for Californian gold miners in the 1850s. Although it was associated with the working class for a long time, denim gradually grew more popular. By the 1970s, women were wearing denim as much as men. In the 1980s, designer jeans were worn by the middle classes and rich, as they are today. Now nearly everyone has at least one piece of clothing made of denim. Unlike its beginnings, it is now _____.

    (a) used to make most jeans
    (b) popular with many workers
    (c) cheaper for everyone to buy
    (d) used in all kinds of fashions

13. Norway and Indonesia will enter into partnership to support Indonesia's efforts to reduce greenhouse gases from deforestation, or the cutting down and burning of forests. Indonesia hopes to reduce its forest-related greenhouse gas emissions with the help of $1 billion in aid from Norway. Indonesia has the third largest forest area in the world but it is losing its forests rapidly. The Norway agreement should change all of that. It is a great step forward in _____.

    (a) creating money from the cutting down of forests
    (b) helping Indonesia's economy grow and prosper
    (c) reducing the tragic loss of large forests
    (d) studying deforestation issues more closely

14. Astronomers have found what they think is _____.
The star originated in the Tarantula Nebula and astronomers think it was ejected into space with a kind of slingshot effect by the gravity of other massive stars. It is moving through space at a record-breaking 400,000 kilometers an hour and has already traveled 375 light-years. But the star's journey will come to an end in half a million years when it is due to explode.

    (a) the fastest nebula system
    (b) a new kind of runaway star
    (c) the remains of an exploded star
    (d) a star with unexplained behavior

15. The Oceans Restaurant in Boston has been serving up great seafood since 1917. It is not a restaurant that tries to do anything too fancy. When you walk into the restaurant, you'll see the decor is old-looking and the tables and chairs are what you might find in your grandmother's kitchen. So the surroundings look a bit cheap. _____, it is quite comfortable and cozy and they don't have to be excessive with the decor. That's not what people go there for—they go for the excellent food.

(a) Similarly
(b) Nonetheless
(c) In addition
(d) As a consequence

16. Two great traditions exist within the religion of Judaism, the Orthodox and Reform branches. While coming from the same origins, Reform and Orthodox Judaism differ in a number of areas. Orthodox Jews have a literal understanding of scriptures and teachings, and are very strict in the beliefs of a literal messiah who is yet to come, a promised land, and a literal life after death. _____, Reform Jews are more conceptual in their approach to scripture and historic teachings. Reform Judaism does not take scriptural texts so literally.

(a) Thus
(b) Moreover
(c) By contrast
(d) To demonstrate

Part II **Questions 17—37**

Read the passage and the question. Then choose the option that best answers the question.

17. Many robots have been sent to Mars from Earth since the 1960s, and now we know a great deal about the planet. We have discovered that the planet is really cold. It is colder than Earth because it is further from the sun and has a thin atmosphere. Its average temperature is -63 degrees C and it can go down to a minimum of -140 degrees C. In many places there is ice under the surface. Mars is the kind of place whose average summer temperature makes a winter in Antarctica seem comfortable.

Q: What is the main idea about Mars in the passage?
(a) Scientists know a lot about it.
(b) It is an extremely cold planet.
(c) Robots have visited it many times.
(d) It is colder than scientists thought.

18. The beverage industry has failed to defeat a soda tax from being introduced in Washington. The industry had succeeded recently against a similar tax in New York. But the Washington Council was more serious about taxing non-diet sodas and has voted in its favor. A soda tax is a good way to raise money to pay for schools and roads. At the same time it can prevent obesity because fewer people will drink soda, which makes people fat perhaps more than anything else. Understandably, the beverage industry is upset by the decision.

Q: What is the main idea of the passage?
(a) Taxes in Washington are increasing.
(b) Fewer people get fat with soda taxes.
(c) Soda taxes upset the beverage industry.
(d) Washington introduced a new tax on sodas.

19. The bad economy has badly affected blacks in Memphis. Not so long ago, Memphis was a place where the rising black working and middle classes had a future to look forward to. But since the recession hit, Memphis blacks have faced rising unemployment and increasing home closures. Two decades of slow progress that increased black wealth and income has been reversed. Incomes of blacks are now back at 1990 levels and home prices continue to fall. The economic divide in Memphis between blacks and whites is increasing.

Q: What is the main idea about Memphis in the passage?
(a) Blacks are losing their homes.
(b) Recession has made blacks poorer.
(c) Blacks are being treated unfairly.
(d) Incomes of blacks have become lower.

20. Many websites are available to consumers who want to complain about companies. Among them are sites like Twitter and Yelp. These give individuals a way to complain to the world about companies that are being dishonest, making a bad product, or maybe just doing something slightly wrong. Through the Web, consumers now have more power. Good corporations realize that if an unhappy customer complains online, it could be bad for business. It is like bad advertising for them.

Q: What is the main idea about consumers in the passage?
(a) They make online businesses worried.
(b) They have the power to complain online.
(c) They complain most about faulty products.
(d) They are making certain websites very popular.

21. The ice of Antarctica is largely untouched and clean. This is perfect for scientists who want to find particles created in the early days of our Solar System. Some scientists have found a few particles after drilling into the ice. When they looked at the chemical makeup of the particles, they could prove that they came from space and have not changed in 4.5 billion years. The little particles may be as old as the sun and are similar to the kinds of particles that come from comets.

Q: What is the passage mainly about?
(a) Analyzing particles from space
(b) Drilling for old comet particles
(c) Looking in Antarctica for space rocks
(d) Finding ancient particles in Antarctica

22. San Francisco was the first city in the U.S. to ban plastic shopping bags. The goal of this was to get people to use reusable bags. The problem with plastic bags is that they get buried in rubbish dumps, where they stay for hundreds of years, or end up in the ocean, where they kill marine animals. But after plastic bags were banned, people started putting groceries into paper bags. This causes environmental problems, too. So now San Francisco authorities want to ban both plastic and paper bags at the check-out counter.

Q: What is the passage on San Francisco mainly about?
(a) People using too many plastic bags
(b) Types of bags shoppers like using
(c) Bans on disposable shopping bags
(d) Authorities against plastic use

23. In 2009, people could go to see a full-scale giant robot based on an anime cartoon standing in Tokyo's Odaiba Shiokaze park. The 20-meter-high giant robot, called a Gundam, had a movable head and shone light from 50 different places within its robot body. The robot was installed in the park in July 2009 to mark the 30th anniversary of a very popular Japanese anime television series called "Mobile Suit Gundam." It was removed in September of 2009 and was erected in the city of Shizuoka in 2010.

Q: Which of the following is correct about the robot according to the passage?
(a) It stands at 30 meters tall.
(b) It moves all parts of its body.
(c) It had been first erected in 2008.
(d) It was taken down to go to Shizuoka.

24. The platypus is a strange mammal that lives in eastern Australia. It makes its home on land next to lakes or rivers where it likes to swim to look for food. For food, it eats worms and water insects. The platypus has webbed feet and looks a little like a beaver, except it also has a duck-billed nose. Platypus can grow to about 30 to 45cms in length. They have furry coats to keep warm. Another strange thing about the platypus is that it lays eggs, instead of giving birth as other mammals do.

Q: Which of the following is correct according to the passage?
(a) The platypus is a kind of mammal.
(b) The platypus does not like water.
(c) The platypus likes to eat leaves.
(d) The platypus grows to 60cm long.

25. The Richat Structure, or Eye of the Sahara, is a large circular formation in the Sahara Desert in Africa. From up in the air, it looks like a giant bull's-eye surrounded by nothing but desert. It is 50 kilometers across and can be seen easily from space, so it has been a special landmark that astronauts have looked at and known about for many years. At first it was thought to have been caused by a meteorite, but now it is thought that the effects of wind and water created it.

Q: Which of the following is correct about the Richat Structure according to the passage?
(a) It is located in South America.
(b) It has a diameter of 50 kilometers.
(c) It was discovered by astronauts recently.
(d) It formed as the result of a meteorite impact.

26. Many people say that the best Western movie ever made was *Stagecoach*, starring John Wayne and directed by John Ford. Cowboy movies were not considered seriously until *Stagecoach* was made and gave a new respectability to the genre. As well as strong characters, the film has many story layers and an exciting plot that includes a spectacular chase scene where Indians attack the stagecoach on a plain. An interesting point of the film is that the supposedly respectable people on the stagecoach turn out to be bad, while the passengers who are looked down on turn out to be good.

Q: Which of the following is correct according to the passage?
(a) *Stagecoach* was spoiled by its weak characters.
(b) Passengers all show a good side in *Stagecoach*.
(c) The movie *Stagecoach* brought respect to Westerns.
(d) A scene with Indians attacking a town appears in *Stagecoach*.

27. Europe's brown bear once lived in the forested areas of the European continent. But farming and hunting since the mid-1800s has reduced the bear's population. The bear is now found in only a few areas in Russia, Scandinavia, Rumania, and Slovenia. The bears used to live across France but disappeared in the 1900s to live only on the slopes of the Pyrénées Mountains. By 1995, only five bears remained in the mountain range, so the French government brought five more from Slovenia and released them on the mountains.

Q: Which of the following is correct according to the passage?
(a) Brown bears live throughout Europe.
(b) Rumania is a home to the brown bear.
(c) Brown bears no longer live in France.
(d) Fewer than five bears live in the Pyrénées.

28. The beautiful Aston Rapide is the kind of car only the very rich can afford. But for all the cost and beauty, it has some faults. The rear seats are so small only a child could be comfortable in them. There is hardly any room in the trunk, either. You could not fit a suitcase. Of course, many sports cars are like that. Another problem, however, is poor visibility for the driver because of the cocoon-like seating and thick roof frame. And amazingly, the navigation system is one of the worst in the car industry.

Q: Which of the following is correct about the Aston Rapide?
(a) Its rear seats are quite roomy.
(b) It has very little luggage storage.
(c) It has good front window visibility.
(d) It comes with the best in electronics.

29. A new species of elephant shrew has been discovered in the remote forests of East Africa. Weighing 700 grams and at about 50 percent heavier than any previously known elephant shrew, it is the largest shrew in the world. This squirrel-size shrew is the only new species of its kind to be discovered in over a century. So far, scientists have learned that it eats insects and lives in damp high-altitude forests. The species is regarded as a "living fossil" because it has not changed much for over 35 million years.

Q: Which of the following is correct about the shrew according to the passage?
(a) It is half the size of other shrews.
(b) Its weight comes to over 900 grams.
(c) It survives by feeding on insects.
(d) Its home is in low-lying areas.

30. In the Middle Ages, men wore tunics down to their knees. Old men and monks wore longer tunics to the ground, as did kings and noblemen at ceremonies. Men sometimes also wore wool pants under their tunics. This was especially true of men in colder areas or who rode horses. Noblemen often wore tights under their tunics. As for women, they all wore at least one tunic down to their ankles. If they could afford it, women also wore a linen under-tunic and a woolen over-tunic. If it was cold, most people wore wool cloaks outside.

Q: Which of the following is correct according to the passage?
(a) Nobles of the Middle Ages never wore tunics.
(b) Men wore wool pants in the Middle Ages.
(c) Only women wore tights in the Middle Ages.
(d) Women of the Middle Ages wore tunics to their knees.

31. The Mr. Coffee J2 is your choice for a great inexpensive coffeemaker. It includes standard features like a pause function, a coffee strength selector, cord storage, and a built-in water filter. But something new to the latest Mr. Coffee J2 is a two-hour automatic shutoff and a cleaning cycle. You won't get that in any other models at the same price. The J2 is built with a strong plastic housing. It also comes with a one-year warranty. If you want a great coffeemaker, the Mr. Coffee J2 is for you!

Q: Which of the following is correct according to the advertisement?
(a) It is expensive to buy the J2.
(b) The J2 shuts off automatically.
(c) The body of the J2 is stainless steel.
(d) The J2 is available with a two-year warranty.

32. There were plenty of tears yesterday as University of Washington's star softball player Denise Ferris ended her softball career. This came after her team, the Huskies, was taken out of the Women's College World Series. Unfortunately, women's softball is a sport with few options after college. Ms. Ferris's choices are now limited to obscure softball leagues here and abroad. Softball is no longer an Olympic sport so playing in the Olympics is not even an option. We will miss her. She was one of the most dominant softball athletes the Northwest has seen.

Q: Which of the following is correct about Ms. Ferris according to the passage?
(a) She played on a Dallas softball team.
(b) She was a star player with the Huskies.
(c) She could not succeed at college softball.
(d) She will possibly play in a future Olympics.

33. Decades ago, "nervous breakdown" was a vague term used by psychiatrists to describe mental problems created by stress or exhaustion. But each generation seems to make its own name for stress-related mental problems. Before the term "nervous breakdown," other names were used, like "melancholia" or "nervous illness." In recent years, psychiatrists have been using the term "burnout syndrome" for people with the same symptoms. Such names seem to come and go depending on what is in fashion.

Q: What can be inferred about "burnout syndrome" from the passage?
(a) It is on the increase.
(b) No one knows what causes it.
(c) It is a new name for an old problem.
(d) Psychiatrists disagree on what it means.

34. By using location data from photographs uploaded online, photographer Eric Fisher created maps of cities showing the places where photographs were taken. He put blue dots where pictures were taken by local residents and red dots where pictures were taken by tourists. In the map of New York, for example, red dots are everywhere near Central Park and Broadway. Blue dots are widely spread across the city. Blue dots are also all over Governors Island, while mostly red dots are on Ellis Island and Liberty Island, where the Statue of Liberty stands.

Q: What can be inferred from the passage?
(a) New Yorkers try to avoid tourists.
(b) Few tourists visit Governors Island.
(c) New York is the world's most photographed city.
(d) Equal numbers of locals and tourists visit Broadway.

35. *The Women Helpers* is a novel about race relations in the Deep South of 1960s America. But it is hard to believe it is a fictional novel because its characters seem so real. They are like friends. Actually, everything in the book is realistic in every detail. The book tells the story of black women who care about others despite an unjust system. It shows how they carry themselves with strength and dignity at all times. This is a beautiful and unforgettable book about fear, courage, love, and suffering.

Q: What can be inferred about the writer?
(a) The writer thinks *The Women Helpers* is true.
(b) The writer enjoyed *The Women Helpers'* humor.
(c) The writer highly recommends *The Women Helpers*.
(d) The writer did not finish reading *The Women Helpers*.

36. What are called premium pet foods cost up to three or four times more than brands found in supermarkets. Also, among the premium brands there is a wide price range. However, they all have the same ingredients since they all have to meet the same nutritional standards. For example, 10 premium chicken dinners for dogs were all found to contain the same ingredients. The non-premium brands use the same ingredients, too, but in different quantities. In fact, the first five ingredients of nearly all cat and dog pet foods are the same.

Q: What can be inferred from the passage?
(a) Many pets lack good nutrition.
(b) Pet foods do not differ greatly.
(c) Quality varies widely in pet foods.
(d) Chicken pet food is the most popular.

37. The Revo hairdryer can dry hair faster and with less heat damage than most other dryers. Not only does it have quick drying speeds, it is also very light and compact. This is the kind of hairdryer you can take anywhere. Its handle can fold to make it even more compact. It can fit in a tiny bag or even the glove compartment of your car. The Revo comes with an attachment so you can actually use it in your car. Professional tests and owner reviews reveal that it is strong and reliable, too.

Q: What can be inferred about the Revo from the passage?
(a) It only has one speed setting.
(b) It is good for traveling.
(c) It is available in many colors.
(d) It costs more than other dryers.

Part III   **Questions 38—40**

Read the passage. Then identify the option that does NOT belong.

38. In past centuries, the quality of life in Europe was determined by the status that one held. (a) This status could not be attained, but depended on which family you were born into. (b) If you were born to a poor family, your life would be one of poverty. (c) The Baltic States have suffered from the highest rates of poverty in Europe. (d) No matter how hard an individual worked, it was impossible to change his or her social situation.

39. Drugs worth millions of dollars have been seized in Sydney by the organized crime squad. (a) Officers executed three search warrants yesterday at premises in a southern Sydney suburb. (b) Officers seized the drugs after they stopped and searched a rental car yesterday. (c) The 28-year-old driver was charged with supplying drugs for an organized crime group. (d) He appeared in court yesterday and was refused bail until his appearance at Sydney's Central Court.

40. If you and your husband cannot think of a name for your baby, take time to sit down and discuss names. (a) Do this as many times as you need and try to pick a time when you are both relaxed. (b) One of the best things to do is for each of you to write a list of ten of your favorite names. (c) Then show each other what you wrote and discuss the names on each list. (d) Some celebrities give their babies strange names, but no one should do that to a child.

This is the end of the Reading Comprehension section. Please remain seated until the proctor has instructed otherwise. You are NOT allowed to turn to any other section of the test.

Actual Test 2

Listening Comprehension 💿

Grammar

Vocabulary

Reading Comprehension

Listening
Comprehension

Part I **Questions 1—15**

You will now hear fifteen conversation fragments, each made up of a single spoken statement followed by four spoken responses. Choose the most appropriate response to the statement.

Part II **Questions 16—30**

You will now hear fifteen conversation fragments, each made up of three spoken statements followed by four spoken responses. Choose the most appropriate response to complete the conversation.

Part III **Questions 31—45**

You will now hear fifteen complete conversations. For each item, you will hear a conversation and its corresponding question, both of which will be read twice. Then you will hear four options which will be read only once. Choose the option that best answers the question.

Part IV **Questions 46—60**

You will now hear fifteen spoken monologues. For each item, you will hear a monologue and its corresponding question, both of which will be read twice. Then you will hear four options which will be read only once. Choose the option that best answers the question.

GRAMMAR

Part I Questions 1—20

Choose the best answer for the blank.

1. A: Ryan is desperately in need of a good frying pan.
   B: Oh, is he? Let me _____.

   (a) find him one
   (b) him find one
   (c) him for find one
   (d) find for one him

2. A: I don't think we can go hiking in this rain!
   B: Yeah, _____.

   (a) I either don't
   (b) I don't either
   (c) either I don't
   (d) either don't I

3. A: You remembered to turn the gas off, right?
   B: Of course, I _____.

   (a) do
   (b) did
   (c) have
   (d) will

4. A: I'm really into reading these days.
   B: What book _____ at the moment?

   (a) will you read
   (b) are you reading
   (c) had you been reading
   (d) having you read

5. A: Please remember to give my message to Nathan.
   B: When I _____ him, I will.

   (a) see
   (b) saw
   (c) will see
   (d) had seen

6. A: Why do you think the new restaurant around the corner is so popular?
   B: They try to make sure every guest _____.

   (a) is felt well taking care of
   (b) feels well to take care of
   (c) felt well taken care of
   (d) feels well taken care of

7. A: Are you sure you have all of the cables _____ correctly?
   B: Trust me. I've been using this equipment for three years.

   (a) connect
   (b) to connect
   (c) connected
   (d) to connecting

8. A: Would you mind reviewing my report for chemistry class?
   B: Of course not. If you're not in _____, I'll do it this weekend.

   (a) hurry
   (b) hurries
   (c) a hurry
   (d) such hurry

9. A: Isn't your cousin dating Jerry Jones?

B: She _____ but they broke up last month.

(a) was going to
(b) used to
(c) would
(d) had

10. A: Susan wrote all her reports in both Japanese and English.

B: That must _____ difficult for her.

(a) being
(b) been
(c) have being
(d) have been

11. A: You know, getting a college education isn't easy.

B: True, but if it were, it _____ be worthless.

(a) will
(b) would
(c) can
(d) should

12. A: I'm really concerned about Derek these days.

B: Yeah, I know. The effects of divorce on a child _____.

(a) be devastated
(b) can be devastating
(c) are to devastate
(d) to be devastated

13. A: Let's keep _____ until someone shows up.

B: No, I think we should call Chris and find out what's going on.

(a) hanging around here
(b) to hang around here
(c) hanging here around
(d) to hang here around

14. A: Have you seen Stan?

B: No, but he _____ in the den.

(a) shall be
(b) can be
(c) might be
(d) need be

15. A: Who were you talking to on the phone?

B: It was Rebecca. She just told me to let you know that she _____.

(a) has arrived early
(b) is early arrived
(c) is arrived early
(d) early has arrived

16. A: Which language do you think you are more fluent in, English or Japanese?

B: Actually, I don't feel like I'm any good at speaking English _____ Japanese.

(a) but
(b) as
(c) yet
(d) or

17. A: Did you find out what happened to the package?

B: They delivered it _____ the wrong address.

(a) on
(b) of
(c) in
(d) to

18. A: I really love my new hobby. It's very enjoyable.

B: So _____.

(a) is mine
(b) be mine
(c) mine is
(d) it is mine

19. A: Why didn't you come to the club last night?

B: I _____, but I had an upset stomach.

(a) wanted
(b) wanted to
(c) wanted to it
(d) wanted to be going

20. A: Why do you always complain that you're so busy?

B: You'll understand _____ you get married and start working full-time.

(a) while
(b) since
(c) even if
(d) once

Part II **Questions 21—40**

Choose the best answer for the blank.

---

21. We would appreciate _____ a catalogue of your products together with some samples.

(a) your sending us
(b) you to send us
(c) for you send us
(d) you are sending us

22. The thieves found _____ the jewelry store and steal some valuable gems.

(a) easy breaking into
(b) to break it into easy
(c) it easy to break into
(d) breaking into easy

23. Not only _____ the equipment, but they also offered their time and efforts in helping us to fight the disease in the remote village.

(a) the group donated
(b) did the group donate
(c) the group had donated
(d) had the group donate

24. A national sports television channel is _____ next year by ABC.

(a) launch
(b) to have launched
(c) to be launched
(d) launched

25. Jasper told his parents that he would take care of _____ from now on.

(a) themselves
(b) himself
(c) oneself
(d) ourselves

26. _____ to go fishing, the boy saw a thunderstorm gathering on the horizon.

(a) To prepare
(b) Being prepared
(c) He was preparing
(d) Preparing

27. Given the current economic slump, this price increase cannot but _____ new sales.

(a) curtail
(b) curtailing
(c) curtailed
(d) be curtailed

28. A healthy life style is the best way to build up _____ to disease.

(a) the resistances
(b) resistance
(c) any resistance
(d) resistances

29. The members of the club are told to invite _____ they want to the summer event.

(a) whomever
(b) whatever
(c) whatsoever
(d) whichever

30. The fire fighter was invited to the school to show _____ in the event of a fire.

(a) the children to do what
(b) the children what to do
(c) what the children do to
(d) what to do the children

31. _____ been wearing a seatbelt, he probably wouldn't have survived the car crash.

(a) He had not
(b) Not had he
(c) Had he not
(d) Were he not

32. Many unlicensed drivers who _____ are illegal immigrants.

(a) have their cars towing
(b) have their cars towed
(c) to have their cars towing
(d) to have their cars towed

33. This table helps you find out how many calories you need _____ to maintain your current weight.

(a) for day
(b) a day
(c) day
(d) the day

34. The only way to gain access to the website is _____ subscribing to the monthly magazine.

(a) for
(b) at
(c) of
(d) by

35. Economists have a _____ brighter outlook on the world economy than before.

    (a) very
    (b) much
    (c) well
    (d) most

36. _____ the moment the scandal broke, the publicist has been trying to cover it up.

    (a) From
    (b) Despite
    (c) For
    (d) During

37. The publisher is looking for _____.

    (a) skilled people at graphic design
    (b) skilled at graphic design people
    (c) people skilled in graphic design
    (d) people in graphic design skilled

38. Brent would rather the girls _____ themselves without bothering him.

    (a) looked after
    (b) looking after
    (c) had looked after
    (d) will look after

39. The mechanic called the woman and said her car is ready _____.

    (a) picking up
    (b) being picked up
    (c) to picking up
    (d) to be picked up

40. Neither of the doctors _____ found the cause of her disease.

    (a) is
    (b) are
    (c) has
    (d) have

Part III **Questions 41—45**

Identify the option that contains an awkward expression or an error in grammar.

41. (a) A: Have you sent the package to Mr. Welch yet?
    (b) B: I didn't know I was supposed to.
    (c) A: Don't you remember me to ask?
    (d) B: Oh, that's right! I'm sorry I forgot.

42. (a) A: Are you going to the charity dinner this Thursday?
    (b) B: I don't know yet. I'm not sure if I were in town.
    (c) A: Oh, really? When will you know for sure?
    (d) B: No later than tomorrow afternoon, I hope.

43. (a) A: I'd like to do something special with my nephews next week.
    (b) B: Why don't you take them to a hiking trip?
    (c) A: Sounds great. My father-in-law has a cabin in the mountains.
    (d) B: You should ask him if it's available to stay in. They'll love it.

44. (a) A: Are you all right? Did you hurt your foot by any chance?
    (b) B: Actually, I sprained my ankle while play soccer yesterday.
    (c) A: Oh, that's too bad. Did you go see a doctor?
    (d) B: Yeah, the doctor told me to stay off my feet for a while.

45. (a) A: Good morning, sir. Are you ready to order?
    (b) B: Yes, I'd like a turkey sandwich and French onion soup, please.
    (c) A: Is that all? Would you like anything to drink?
    (d) B: Umm, can I get small lemonade, too?

Part IV Questions 46—50

Identify the option that contains an awkward expression or an error in grammar.

46. (a) Dogs have a great sense of smell and some of them are used to help sniff out drugs and bombs. (b) Charlie is one particular dog whose job is to find mold in homes, businesses, and other areas. (c) When he smells mold nearby, he sits down to let human know that he has detected mold. (d) He really helps people because mold can be dangerous and can make people sick.

47. (a) Many people can develop travel problems because their airplanes either arrive late or cannot depart on time. (b) It is a common problem which is only getting worse for travelers at airports around the world. (c) A major cause for delays are weather, such as fog, thunderstorms, or icy conditions that make runways slippery. (d) It is unfortunate that weather creates about 70% of delays at airports but there is no solution for it.

48. (a) Just like in other places, people who live in Elmwood want to build bigger but better houses. (b) However, property there is expensive and many people cannot afford the high prices. (c) Owners want to tear down or move houses so that others can build on the lots that are available. (d) Some property owners have decided to leave and give up their houses to people in poorer neighborhoods.

49. (a) Peershare is a computer software company that allows users to copy music by sharing files online. (b) Millions of people have enjoyed downloading as much music as they want from Peershare without paying a cent. (c) But musicians and the recording industry are against Peershare and want to shut it down. (d) They are protesting that they lose money when users are allowed copy music for free.

50. (a) A lot of research goes into finding a cure for AIDS so the medicines to treat AIDS cost a lot of money. (b) Unfortunately, in Africa, many people who develop AIDS do not have enough money to afford expensive drugs. (c) However, in recent years, considerable energy and money has gone into trying to give universal access to AIDS treatment. (d) One effort involves just one man who is helping sick Africans for paying for the medication out of his own pocket.

This is the end of the Grammar section. Do NOT move on to the next section until instructed to do so. You are NOT allowed to turn to any other section of the test.

VOCABULARY

DIRECTIONS

This part of the exam tests your vocabulary skills. You will have
15 minutes to complete the 50 questions. Be sure to follow the
directions given by the proctor.

Part I Questions 1—25

Choose the best answer for the blank.

1. A: What is the population of Delhi?

B: I'm not sure, but I know it's one of the most _____ populated cities in the world.

(a) largely
(b) densely
(c) mainly
(d) roughly

2. A: The President showed real courage and leadership in his decision.

B: That's why people _____ him.

(a) come out with
(b) do away with
(c) hang on to
(d) look up to

3. A: Are these new women's fashions by Vicky?

B: Yes. I like them because they are stylish and the prices are _____.

(a) unreasonable
(b) prohibitive
(c) outrageous
(d) affordable

4. A: You're late again! I always have to wait for you!

B: That's not always the _____.

(a) accident
(b) case
(c) issue
(d) fact

5. A: If you can believe it, the _____ for renewing your license is $75.

B: Are you kidding me? That's absurd.

(a) prize
(b) charge
(c) premium
(d) fine

6. A: Your meal was perfect. I enjoyed every part of it.

B: Thanks for the _____.

(a) brag
(b) display
(c) notification
(d) compliment

7. A: Excuse me. I'd like to see Dr. Bruno.

B: You may if you have a(n) _____.

(a) appointment
(b) promise
(c) timetable
(d) commitment

8. A: What happened? This room is a mess!

B: Don't look at me like that. It's not my _____.

(a) guilt
(b) fault
(c) defect
(d) blame

9. A: Do you know where the convention is being held?

    B: No, I don't know the _____, either.

    (a) position
    (b) venue
    (c) orientation
    (d) placement

10. A: Wow! Dale, you look _____.

    B: Thanks. I've been working out recently.

    (a) generous
    (b) down
    (c) fit
    (d) exhausted

11. A: Are you not going to eat that bacon?

    B: My doctor ordered me to _____ on animal fat.

    (a) throw up
    (b) dish out
    (c) cut back
    (d) hang up

12. A: I really _____ your assistance.

    B: I'm happy to be of help.

    (a) appraise
    (b) appreciate
    (c) apprise
    (d) apprehend

13. A: The new student is so _____.

    B: Yeah, she's definitely a little different, but I don't mind her.

    (a) loose
    (b) weird
    (c) stable
    (d) average

14. A: Hello, can I talk to Ms. Brown?

    B: Please hold the _____ and I'll connect you with her.

    (a) call
    (b) phone
    (c) line
    (d) minute

15. A: Do you know how to _____ the size of a photo with this software?

    B: Yes, it is actually easy to blow up photos.

    (a) gain
    (b) resize
    (c) elongate
    (d) increase

16. A: You two make a great couple! How did you two meet?

    B: She _____ my eye one day while walking down the street.

    (a) kept
    (b) lighted
    (c) fascinated
    (d) caught

17. A: Would you like a(n) _____ seat or a window seat on this flight?

    B: It doesn't matter to me.

    (a) row
    (b) door
    (c) open
    (d) aisle

18. A: I'll give you a _____ to the hospital.

B: Thank you, but I'll just take a cab.

(a) lift
(b) height
(c) boost
(d) hand

19. A: You did really well in the conference. Everyone liked your speech.

B: Thanks, but at first I was on _____ and needles.

(a) studs
(b) threads
(c) nails
(d) pins

20. A: Mom, can I stay over at Jim's house tonight?

B: That's out of the _____. It's a school night.

(a) mind
(b) stock
(c) question
(d) order

21. A: Do you speak any other languages besides English?

B: Yes. I'm fluent in Spanish and have a _____ knowledge of French.

(a) working
(b) low
(c) making
(d) delicate

22. A: Do you realize how expensive toothpaste is?

B: Yeah, the prices of personal _____ products have soared recently.

(a) lavatory
(b) clearance
(c) hygiene
(d) salutation

23. A: Don't you think he was acting quite rude last night?

B: Yeah, his behavior made many people _____ at the party.

(a) distorted
(b) retarded
(c) uncomfortable
(d) incomprehensible

24. A: I'm sorry I lost my _____ last night.

B: That's all right. I understand.

(a) understanding
(b) reason
(c) temper
(d) thought

25. A: I'd like a room with an ocean _____, please.

B: I'm afraid they are all occupied.

(a) look
(b) sight
(c) view
(d) appearance

Part II **Questions 26—50**

Choose the best answer for the blank.

26. We invested a large amount of money to create a safe working _____.

(a) environment
(b) surroundings
(c) circumstances
(d) atmosphere

27. Studies show that lack of sleep may _____ to obesity.

(a) procure
(b) adjust
(c) react
(d) contribute

28. A group of scientists will _____ some experiments to test the new vaccine.

(a) play
(b) perform
(c) act
(d) behave

29. His paintings never gained the international _____ they deserved during his lifetime.

(a) recognition
(b) bid
(c) offer
(d) demise

30. The new car Brad wanted was too _____ so he had to buy something cheaper.

(a) rich
(b) costly
(c) worthy
(d) valuable

31. The prime minister vowed to lower the nation's unemployment rate to 3 percent during his four-year _____.

(a) semester
(b) time
(c) quarter
(d) term

32. The young man rose through the _____ to become a top executive of his organization.

(a) phases
(b) degrees
(c) ranks
(d) steps

33. More than 1 million people have been able to _____ the smoking habit with the help of a nicotine patch.

(a) bring
(b) break
(c) retain
(d) leak

34. The _____ of a good education is that it gives you a head start with your career.

(a) lesson
(b) interest
(c) pitfall
(d) advantage

35. According to the manager, the band's third album is _____ out this March.

    (a) near
    (b) way
    (c) due
    (d) able

36. The committee members tried to _____ him into accepting the proposal but he wouldn't listen.

    (a) talk
    (b) ask
    (c) tell
    (d) discuss

37. *The Herald* has _____ a lawsuit against a company it claims is flooding its computer network with spam mail.

    (a) filed
    (b) asked
    (c) shot
    (d) registered

38. The program aims to _____ domestic violence especially in poor countries in Southeast Asia and Africa.

    (a) address
    (b) harass
    (c) impress
    (d) express

39. Every year, the FBI releases its official list of the top ten most wanted _____ who are on the loose.

    (a) reformers
    (b) policies
    (c) criminals
    (d) debutants

40. Please provide us with a(n) _____ from your previous employer along with your résumé and a cover letter.

    (a) perspective
    (b) reference
    (c) digestive
    (d) avarice

41. In 2009, numerous construction companies went bankrupt in the wake of worldwide inflation _____ by high oil prices.

    (a) fired
    (b) sparked
    (c) pricked
    (d) dulled

42. Stan _____ when he finally got promoted after five years of hard work at the company.

    (a) exulted
    (b) exacted
    (c) executed
    (d) exempted

43. There was no local _____ in circulation in Zimbabwe for much of 2009.

    (a) currency
    (b) finance
    (c) payment
    (d) accounts

44. It is a good thing to have a true friend in whom one can always _____.

    (a) confound
    (b) confide
    (c) conform
    (d) confront

45. After years of consulting startup businesses, he became extremely _____ at accounting and finance.

(a) adept
(b) ambiguous
(c) tricky
(d) tenuous

46. Since news of their _____ with local politicians broke out, the company has been under investigation for tax evasion.

(a) route
(b) election
(c) blister
(d) collusion

47. The activist is urging governments to help _____ the famine in sub-Saharan nations.

(a) alleviate
(b) exacerbate
(c) envisage
(d) allege

48. She _____ from her prepared speech to pay tribute to the President before getting back to the point.

(a) leapt
(b) missed
(c) retorted
(d) digressed

49. Constructing a building higher than a two-story house in this area without permission from the city is a _____ of the Greenbelt Act.

(a) boost
(b) ballot
(c) breach
(d) brink

50. A group of directors and actors staged a protest against the government's increased _____ of movies.

(a) protection
(b) salute
(c) censorship
(d) rupture

This is the end of the Vocabulary section. Do NOT move on to the Reading Comprehension section until instructed to do so. You are NOT allowed to turn to any other section of the test.

READING
COMPREHENSION

Part I   **Questions 1—16**

Read the passage. Then choose the option that best completes the passage.

---

1. Teachers are expected to be knowledgeable about the subjects they teach. In
    addition, there are some personal traits that are desirable in teachers. High on that
    list is an engaging personality. Teachers need to hold the attention of students. They
    should not be melancholy, timid, or reserved. That is because students do not learn
    when they are uninspired. It is also essential for a teacher to have sympathy for
    students. They should have a capacity to understand the minds and feelings of other
    people. So, they need to be _____.

    (a) knowledgeable of many other subjects
    (b) committed to teaching for a long time
    (c) intelligent enough to learn the job
    (d) tolerant of children's immaturity

2. Alaska's Iditarod Trail Sled Dog Race is one of the world's longest and most
    difficult races. Starting in Anchorage, huskies have to pull sleds across the snow
    and ice to Nome, Alaska. The teams _____. It usually
    takes them eight to fifteen days to reach the finish line. On average, more than fifty
    sleds start the race. Each sled team consists of about 16 dogs. Teams will often race
    through blizzards. They have to endure extreme temperatures and gale-force winds.
    Sometimes this can make the surrounding air feel as cold as -70°C.

    (a) cover a distance of 1,868 kilometers
    (b) train a long time for the short race
    (c) finish the race within a week
    (d) consist of huskies instead

3. Chavacano, a language spoken by some people in the Philippines,
    _____. Usage depends on the level of familiarity
    between the speaker and the addressee; the status of both in family and society;
    or the mood of the speaker and addressee at the particular moment. The pronouns
    used by speakers can be common, familiar, or formal. The common forms can be
    used among peers since they convey no formality or courtesy in conversation. The
    common forms can also imply crudeness, impoliteness, or hostility.

    (a) makes sense to most French speakers
    (b) uses three different levels of pronouns
    (c) is harder to learn than other languages
    (d) is used by certain mountain tribes

4. Thank you for purchasing an Electro Times warranty. This warranty protects you for one year. It starts on the day you buy your product. If the product breaks, we will repair it for you. You will not need to pay for the repair. We will also cover your shipping costs. If we cannot repair the product, we will send you a replacement. Please keep this warranty in a safe place. If there are problems with your product, you will need to send a copy. Without it you cannot

_____ .

(a) have your order delivered quickly
(b) obtain a warranty to cover your product
(c) have your product repaired or replaced
(d) provide us with all details of your problem

5.

Dear Constance,

I adopted a kitten that _____ . Max was fun to have around at the beginning. However, I'm having difficulties with him now. He jumps on me early in the morning, pees on the carpet, etc. I know these things are not his fault. Still, they are really annoying. My job is making me busier and I have less time and patience for him, too. I don't want to abandon Max, but I regret that I adopted him more and more each day. What should I do? Please help!

Regards,
Sheila

(a) has become a problem
(b) my boyfriend doesn't like
(c) bothers the cats around him
(d) takes up too much of my time

6. Flying squirrels do not have wings. And they don't actually fly. They glide. These rodents have a stretchy, cape-like skin that allows them to glide through the air. Some can glide up to a distance of 90 meters. Flying squirrels conduct most of their activities at night. In the wild, they can be expected to live about five years. However, _____. This is because they are not preyed upon by other creatures, most notably spotted owls.

   (a) life in the wild can be dangerous
   (b) it depends on how much they breed
   (c) their life span can double in captivity
   (d) they sometimes appear during daytime

7. Cell phone use _____. Even a good driver turns into an idiot when a cell phone goes up to the ear. Drivers who talk on cell phones become unaware of their surroundings. They put themselves and others in danger. Drivers who use cell phones are three to four times more likely to be in a crash. Using a hands-free device does not improve the situation and still distracts the driver. Drivers should pull over to the side of the road, park the car, and then use their cell phone.

   (a) has increased on the road dramatically
   (b) magnifies the stupidity of a driver
   (c) is rising while driving is on the decline
   (d) is a necessary evil nowadays

8. Jupiter is the largest planet in the solar system. Its volume is 1,300 times greater than the Earth's. Unlike Earth, it does not have a solid surface. Scientists believe that it is made of gases and fluids consisting of hydrogen, helium, ammonia, and methane. The interior of Jupiter might be liquid hydrogen. Usually, hydrogen is a gas, but Jupiter's deep interior is under immense pressure. This may cause the hydrogen to _____.

   (a) create new elements like carbon and cobalt
   (b) be compressed and become a liquid
   (c) slightly expand the size of Jupiter
   (d) remain a gas in the atmosphere

9. We hope you enjoy your visit to Terra. We make food from fresh, locally grown ingredients. Our upstairs restaurant serves a fixed-course menu. Or if you prefer, you can order à la carte from our downstairs café menu. We strive to choose the very best produce in season for our meals. The majority of our ingredients _____. Our meats come from the nearby Berkshire Estate and most of our fruits and vegetables are produced by Froghollow just outside the city. We believe that dining is more than just food on a plate.

(a) come from wherever they are in season
(b) are sold at supermarkets nationwide
(c) have been organically grown by us
(d) are from local farms and suppliers

10. Walking on the sidewalks of downtown Toronto can be a frustrating experience. Most of the space is devoted to vehicles. The streets for traffic are wide. This leaves just a narrow strip for pedestrians. People on foot must share this space with restaurant patios, garbage bins, street vendors, and tourists. It can be chaotic. Obstacles make it difficult for people _____.

(a) to get a decent parking spot in the city
(b) to drive around Toronto comfortably
(c) to avoid spilling over into the street
(d) to find a decent restaurant to eat at

11. An education panel has _____ at the P.S. 92 school. Ms. Kim, the teacher in question, had been fired for teaching evolutionary theory. The panel says science teacher Marsha Kim will return to P.S. 92 over parents' objections. Dashell Terrone, one of the panel members, says Ms. Kim was within her right to teach evolution. P.S. 92 is not a religious school, but many families in the area are conservative Christians. Manuel Carter, the principal at P.S. 92 who let Ms. Kim go, says that while he does not agree he respects the panel's decision.

(a) kicked an teacher out
(b) criticized an instructor
(c) commended a professor
(d) reinstated a school teacher

12. Many people say that you should look on the bright side. That might sound like hollow advice sometimes, but it turns out that it may help you live longer. According to a new study, _____. It found that cheery women were significantly less likely to die of cancers or any other diseases than depressed ones. The same results also came from men. The findings show that optimistic people seem to seek medical advice and follow it, and have more friends that help them deal with stress.

(a) the same is true for most pessimistic people
(b) pessimistic women tend to eat well but sleep poorly
(c) optimists have a lower risk of cancer and early death
(d) optimistic women are healthier than their male counterparts

13. At Aromatico, our goal is to provide the best possible coffee to people around the world. We use infrared sensors to weed out immature beans. We also believe that freshness is essential to great coffee, so after we roast our coffee beans we place them in vacuum packed stainless steel containers. This method assures that the beans remain in the best possible condition before opening. You might think _____. Once you try our coffee, however, you'll taste the difference immediately and realize why.

(a) good coffee can't be this cheap
(b) making instant coffee is all we do
(c) growing coffee this way is unusual
(d) we go to extremes to bring you coffee

14. King Soda's brand in the diet cola wars used to be called Diet Cola. However, it was behind Diet Rite from Royal Crown Cola. When Donald Jones became the CEO of King Soda, he made a bold decision. Instead of distancing diet sodas from their full-calorie drinks, he renamed Diet Cola in 1963. Its new name was Diet King. King Soda became the first large pop company to give its diet line the same name as its main product. The move was so successful that _____.

(a) Donald Jones joined Royal Crown Cola
(b) King Cola's sales went through the roof
(c) Diet Rite became the number one soft drink
(d) other companies finally brought out diet sodas

15. Today, most countries in the Pacific are democracies. In 1945, though, only a few were. At the end of World War II, many Pacific nations' economies were in ruins. Now, they are strong and productive. _____, we cannot forget that old conflicts and new competition for resources could threaten what has been built up the last 70 years. Cooperation can help prevent that. Working together will ultimately be more fruitful than working against each other.

    (a) Thus
    (b) Still
    (c) Therefore
    (d) Furthermore

16. When Barack Obama was campaigning to become President, he made his daughters Sasha and Malia a promise: he would get the girls a dog if he was elected. President Obama kept his promise. _____, he let the girls have a Portuguese dog named Bo when he won the election. The dog was a gift from Senator Edward Kennedy. Bo was named in honor of First Lady Michelle Obama's father's nickname.

    (a) Indeed
    (b) Despite this
    (c) However
    (d) In addition

17. Parents may give their children an allowance, sometimes for doing extra work around the house. Some children earn a weekly allowance while others earn it monthly. It helps the child learn the value of money. The children are then expected to buy their own things with their allowance. The goal is to show young people how to save and spend. Saving helps children understand that some purchases require sacrifice. They learn that they should not spend all their money at once. They have to cut costs and plan for the future.

Q: What is the best title for the passage?
(a) Teach Kids How to Earn Money
(b) Pay Your Children Money for Work
(c) Allowances Are Healthy for Your Children
(d) Kids Can Learn about Money with Allowances

18. Robert Chase hopes to help people by developing snake-like robots. He hopes they can search for victims by sliding through small spaces. The robots have cameras and electronic sensors. Their delicate movements can be controlled with a joystick. It is important that the robots are small. They need to maneuver through fallen buildings and climb pipes. Chase's robots are about the size of a human arm or smaller. In natural disasters like earthquakes or tsunamis, snake robots can help rescuers find injured people.

Q: What is the passage mainly about?
(a) Snake-like robots made to rescue
(b) Robots taught to behave like a snake
(c) The development of snake-like robots
(d) The working principles of snake-like robots

19. The railroad was an important development for society. It followed a schedule. Thus, it made precise timekeeping important. However, it was not the first system to do so. Throughout history merchants have been selling items at daybreak. People have also been celebrating events together. This means that they roughly agreed with their neighbors as to the time of day. Society needs to agree on the time. Or else everyday life would be a mess.

Q: What is the main idea of the passage?
(a) Some of our traditions are timeless.
(b) Timekeeping has an ancient history.
(c) The railroad helped people follow a schedule.
(d) An accepted way of measuring time is necessary.

20. Buying from an online auction site like My Auction is simple. Some items have a fixed price for users to buy right away. If the item is being auctioned, you offer the highest price you are prepared to pay. Then My Auction bids for you. Others may bid more than you. If that happens, you are emailed and asked if you would like to bid again. Auctions last up to 10 days. When they are over you get an email telling you whether you have won the item. Most buyers pay for their items with PayPal, an online payment system.

Q: What is the passage mainly about?
(a) The ways of increasing an auction bid
(b) The advantages of an online-auction site
(c) The way to use an online-auction system
(d) The convenience of making online payments

21. Youth sports injuries are a growing problem. Only professional athletes used to have severe injuries. But now high school and even junior high athletes are getting them. There are many reasons behind the increase. Mainly, youth sports have become extremely organized and parents, volunteers, and coaches can be very demanding. They emphasize training and competing for the top spot. Sometimes they can produce Olympic athletes. However, the repeated training places enormous stresses on bones and muscles.

Q: What is the best title for the news report?
(a) The Participation in Organized Sports by Children
(b) The Common Occurrence of Youth Sports Injuries
(c) The Way to Train Children in Organized Sports
(d) The Main Causes of Youth Sports Injuries

22. Alfred Nobel was a Swedish chemist. When he died he donated his money to create the Nobel Prize, which is awarded in five categories: chemistry, physics, medicine, literature, and peace. Nobel Committees send invitations to hundreds of scientists and scholars. They ask them to suggest names for the Nobel Prizes. When received, each committee discusses the suggested names and makes a short list of possible winners. A vote is taken for the prizewinner. The Nobel Peace Prize is presented at Oslo University, while other prizes are given at a ceremony in Stockholm. Each Nobel winner gives a Nobel lecture when claiming the prize.

Q: What is the passage mainly about?
(a) The Nobel Prize winners in different fields
(b) The organization of the Nobel Committee
(c) The work done by a Swedish scientist
(d) The background of the Nobel Prize

23. There are more than 1,000 kinds of catfish. One kind found in Florida is called the walking catfish. It has an extra lung for breathing on dry land. When its swimming hole dries up, the walking catfish leaves the hole and uses its front fins to crawl to another lake or stream. Another kind is the armored catfish. It gets its name from the heavy, bony plates protecting its body. Some armored catfish weighing over 100 pounds have been found in South America. However, most catfish are much smaller.

Q: Which of the following is correct according to the passage?
(a) Florida has 1,000 types of catfish.
(b) Walking catfish walk on two front legs.
(c) Armored catfish have bodily protection.
(d) South America is home to only small catfish.

24. Sometimes a company has hard times. Several events can lead it toward a downward spiral. Slow sales can make employees lose hope. Talented workers leave, new programs are delayed, and sales suffer even more. Astra seems to be headed for a downward spiral. It has all the symptoms: loss of profits, unpopular products, and fleeing employees. A closer look shows that Astra's costs are higher than their competitors. They also produce less than their competitors. And finally, they are not creating new products that people want.

Q: Which of the following is correct about Astra according to the passage?
(a) It has experienced a pick-up in sales.
(b) It is not able to retain good employees.
(c) It has recently cut down on high spending.
(d) It is outdoing competitors with popular products.

25. It can be difficult to deal with your anger when someone hurts you deeply. But it is possible to forgive. Research shows that forgiveness is helpful to your physical and mental health. People who are able to forgive say they have more energy and better sleep patterns. Dr. Frederic Luskin is a psychologist and the author of *Forgive for Good*. He says that holding onto wrongs that people have done blocks our happiness and makes it impossible to get on with our lives.

Q: According to the passage, what is the right way to calm down after being hurt?
(a) Figure out why you got hurt
(b) Confront the person who hurt you
(c) Forgive what others have done to you
(d) Think about doing good and not bad things

26.

Dear Governor Rosedale,

I am writing to oppose the state's landfill project in Clifton Woods. The potential harm of this facility far outweighs the benefits. We do not need or want a garbage complex of this size in the area. The region offers great opportunities for outdoor recreation. People like to hike, camp, and fish there. Every visitor comments on the peace and beauty of Clifton Woods' natural environment. They do not want to smell trash and hear garbage trucks. Please preserve this region for its forest and wildlife.

Sincerely,
Daniel Verdun

Q: Which of the following is correct according to the letter?
(a) The state plans to clean up Clifton Woods.
(b) The wildlife is damaging the local park lands.
(c) The Clifton Woods area attracts many skiers.
(d) The government wants to build a garbage dump.

27. The City Building Education Program is a program for students from kindergarten through the 12th grade. It uses the stages of city planning to teach reading, writing, and math. Children map and analyze what their own district needs. They look at the housing, transportation, and energy requirements. An architect visits the classroom once a week. With his aid, the students can think of new ways to meet the needs of the city. They can also build models of their creations. CBEP helps children with problem-solving. They observe, analyze, and work on possible solutions.

Q: Why does an architect pay a weekly visit to the classroom?
(a) To plan lessons with the teacher
(b) To assist kids with their program
(c) To hear creative ideas from the students
(d) To give children lectures about architecture

28. Maté, pronounced "mah-tay," is a South American drink. It is prepared by steeping dry leaves and twigs of yerba maté in hot water. Traditionally, the cup is shared among close friends and family members. The people drink it using the same straw. The author Robert Heinlein wrote about "water brothers," people who become closer when they drink from the same glass. Similarly, those who share the maté cup have a bond. They share the health and meditation of yerba maté. Thus, it becomes a sign of acceptance and friendship.

Q: Which of the following is correct according to the passage?
(a) Making yerba maté is achieved using iced water.
(b) Yerba maté is drunk in one-shot from a glass.
(c) Drinking maté is a means of social bonding.
(d) Maté does not have any health properties.

29. Spain colonized the Florida peninsula in the 1500s. However, Native Americans in Florida and English colonists challenged Spain in the 1600s. Spain lost Florida when Britain gained control of the area in 1763. Florida was returned to Spain 20 years later, after the British were defeated in the American Revolution. But Americans wanted control of Florida. In 1819, Spain and the US signed the Florida Purchase Treaty. In the treaty, Spain agreed to hand over the remainder of Florida to the United States.

Q: Which of the following is correct according to the passage?
(a) Florida was colonized in the 1600s.
(b) Florida came under US control in 1763.
(c) Britain controlled Florida for two decades.
(d) Britain and the US signed a treaty over Florida.

30. Children of all ages and many adults love to play with toys and games. These could be dolls, action figures, board games, or stuffed animals. This website is devoted to the history of toys. In the History section, you can learn about the origin of these toys. In the Memories section, readers share their memories of their favorite toys. Go back in time to your childhood and relive the joy of playing. Whether you are discovering new toys or remembering past ones, everyone can have fun on this site.

Q: Which of the following is correct about the site according to the passage?
(a) It is primarily set up for online gamers.
(b) Members are able to chat with others about toys.
(c) Users can learn about popular toys and games in history.
(d) Children and adults are able to purchase many popular games.

31. Burning Man is an annual festival. It ends in September on the Labor Day holiday in the United States. The festival takes place in the Black Rock Desert, about 90 miles from Reno, Nevada. However, the specific location can change from year to year. In addition to being a festival, Burning Man is a social experiment. Community, self-expression, and radical concepts are emphasized. Everyone is encouraged to participate. Burning Man gets its name from a special ritual in which the festival goers burn a large wooden sculpture of a man.

Q: Which of the following is correct according to the passage?
(a) The festival takes place in Reno, Nevada.
(b) Burning Man is strictly an invitation-only event.
(c) The festival is held annually at the same location.
(d) Attendees burn a wooden figure during the festival.

32. As a theater critic, I have seen hundreds of performances. In particular, I have seen many productions of *Into the Sea*. It is based on the book of the same title. The story is a familiar love story that has been told many times. That is why I was delighted by the Holbrook Theater's recent production. It brought new life to this old story. Most other productions stick to the book's storyline. I have never before seen attempts to modernize it. The Holbrook Theater director, Hans Merchant, has done a terrific job.

Q: Which is correct about the production of *Into the Sea*?
(a) It interprets *Into the Sea* in a new light.
(b) It is shown in a newly renovated theater.
(c) It is delightful and true to the original work.
(d) It falls short of Hans Merchant's usual standard.

33. From colonial times to the beginning of the 19th century, most goods were transported by water in the United States. Goods were produced in one place and then sent by ship to be sold in another place. Some goods moved over rough roads, but areas lacking roads had to have goods transported by pack horse. This method of transport often cost more than the goods themselves. The manufacturers and politicians at the time tried to solve this problem. The developments they planned required large sums of money but they knew that it would pay off.

Q: What can be inferred about early US history from the passage?
(a) Trading in goods resulted in improved land transport.
(b) Before the 19th century, many merchants lost money.
(c) Goods transportation was hindered by Native Americans.
(d) Water transport became more expensive than road transport.

34. One lawmaker in California wants chain restaurants to put nutritional information on their menus, and the U.S. Congress is deciding on bills that protect restaurants from obesity-related lawsuits. This raises the question: are restaurants responsible for the health of their customers? Fast-food restaurants say they are not the only ones with high calorie meals. They want other establishments, not just fast-food and chain restaurants, to reveal information. If these bills pass, we may soon see details on calorie, fat, and sodium content alongside prices on menus.

Q: What can be inferred from the passage?
(a) The U.S. will cease being the country with the fattest people.
(b) Restaurants have started adding nutritional information on menus.
(c) Some diners blame fast-food restaurants for their health problems.
(d) The Californian lawmaker became obese after eating at chain restaurants.

35. Depression is a mental health disorder. It can affect many things in your life such as the way you eat, sleep, and think about things. A common sign of depression is losing interest in activities you previously enjoyed. Now science is hoping to use music to treat depression. In a new study, Canadian researchers studied people who were recently diagnosed with depression and how music creates changes in the brain. When they studied brain scans of the people in the study as they listened to their favorite music, the results proved interesting.

Q: What is likely to follow in this news report?
(a) The symptoms of depression
(b) The music listened to in the study
(c) A possible new cure for depression
(d) A description of changes seen in the brain

36. A study of British detectives found that they spent just a few hours a day at home. UK detectives work twelve hours a day, almost every day of the week. Their training is also rigorous. After sixteen weeks of basic training, the detective enters the force. He must then complete two trial years. Then he can join the Criminal Investigation Department on a trial basis. After two years of good service there he can become a detective constable. All of this affects their marriages, and they have the highest divorce rate of any profession.

Q: What can be inferred about detectives in the UK?
(a) Many fail the training phase because it is too hard.
(b) They receive stricter training than in other countries.
(c) Many risk their lives unnecessarily in the line of duty.
(d) They spend less time with their families than other people.

37. Etiquette is more than knowing whether your bread plate goes on the left or right side of your dinner plate. It is about how you present yourself. Having good etiquette shows that you are comfortable around people. So, during a business lunch it is important to have good etiquette. Clients want to be able to trust you. They want to know that you have consideration for others. For them, your etiquette shows a level of maturity and sophistication. Many business deals have failed because someone did not have the proper manners.

Q: What can be inferred from the passage?
(a) Some people are uncomfortable paying too much attention to etiquette.
(b) Business etiquette is essentially about copying others' manners.
(c) Showing poor etiquette could lead to the loss of a job.
(d) Good etiquette guarantees your success in business.

Part III **Questions 38 — 40**

Read the passage. Then identify the option that does NOT belong.

38. The telephone is an important tool used every day to communicate with people all over the world. (a) The first practical telephone was invented in the 1870s by Alexander Graham Bell. (b) He filed a patent for it, and his competitor, Elisha Gray, filed a similar patent just a few hours afterwards. (c) Bell was born in Edinburgh, Scotland, on March 3, 1847, and moved to Canada and then to the U.S. (d) But Bell was the one the U.S. Patent Office awarded with the first patent for a telephone.

39. Blood Falls is located at the tip of a giant glacier in Victoria Land, East Antarctica. (a) It gets its name not from actual blood but the water there that is rich in iron. (b) When the water trickles out from underground, the iron reacts with the air and quickly forms red rust. (c) It has been found that microbes live in this inhospitable and icy environment on sulfur and iron compounds. (d) The water itself probably comes from an underground lake that has a high concentration of salt.

40. No one really knows where the first tomato was grown. (a) Tomatoes are widespread and have been grown in many countries for centuries. (b) Wild tomatoes can be found throughout South America and the remote areas of the Galapagos Islands. (c) So, finding out exactly where the first tomato originated is not always easy to do. (d) According to one scientist, the area which still has the highest variety is often the origin.

This is the end of the Reading Comprehension section. Please remain seated until the proctor has instructed otherwise. You are NOT allowed to turn to any other section of the test.

Actual Test 3

TEPS

LISTENING COMPREHENSION

Part I **Questions 1—15**

You will now hear fifteen conversation fragments, each made up of a single spoken statement followed by four spoken responses. Choose the most appropriate response to the statement.

Part II **Questions 16—30**

You will now hear fifteen conversation fragments, each made up of three spoken statements followed by four spoken responses. Choose the most appropriate response to complete the conversation.

Part III   **Questions 31—45**

You will now hear fifteen complete conversations. For each item, you will hear a conversation and its corresponding question, both of which will be read twice. Then you will hear four options which will be read only once. Choose the option that best answers the question.

Part IV   **Questions 46—60**

You will now hear fifteen spoken monologues. For each item, you will hear a monologue and its corresponding question, both of which will be read twice. Then you will hear four options which will be read only once. Choose the option that best answers the question.

GRAMMAR

Part I   Questions 1—20

Choose the best answer for the blank.

1. A: It was stressful to spend so much
       time with Matt yesterday.
    B: I find _____ at times myself.

    (a) hard to take him
    (b) him hard to take
    (c) it hard to take
    (d) him hard to take it

2. A: Do you think Sally will accept the
       proposal?
    B: I'm not sure, _____.

    (a) I hope
    (b) hoping so
    (c) so I hope it
    (d) but I hope so

3. A: I'm confused. What should I do
       regarding Barbara?
    B: If I were you, _____ to her.

    (a) I'll apologize
    (b) I'd apologize
    (c) I'd apologized
    (d) I'd have apologized

4. A: Have you ever been to India?
    B: Yes, I _____ to Delhi three
       years ago.

    (a) had traveled
    (b) would travel
    (c) traveled
    (d) have traveled

5. A: Do you like the new Chief
       Information Officer?
    B: Yes, I find her very easy to

       _____.

    (a) talk
    (b) talk to
    (c) be talked
    (d) be talked with

6. A: The Royal Circus _____ to
       the Art Center in Sacramento. Are
       you interested in seeing it?
    B: Yes, I love the circus!

    (a) has come
    (b) is coming
    (c) had come
    (d) came

7. A: Sorry, but it's not your turn, sir.
    B: I thought I _____, though.

    (a) called my name to hear
    (b) heard my name calling
    (c) called my name hearing
    (d) heard my name called

8. A: When do you plan _____ a
       new store?
    B: Probably in the next five or six
       months.

    (a) to open
    (b) opening
    (c) to opening
    (d) on opening with

9. A: _____ in Buenos Aires?
    B: Hold on. Let me check my schedule.

    (a) Will you be staying until what time
    (b) Until what time will you be staying
    (c) Until what time you will be staying
    (d) What time you will be staying until

10. A: The presentation was horrible, wasn't it?
    B: I don't think it _____ any worse.

    (a) should be
    (b) ought to be
    (c) had better be
    (d) could have been

11. A: I'm worried about our hiking trip to Milford Sound next week because of the storm warnings.
    B: If I were you, I would delay _____ the weather clears up.

    (a) by
    (b) until
    (c) as
    (d) when

12. A: Do you have a room with a great view?
    B: Yes. Would you like a room _____ the beach?

    (a) to face
    (b) facing
    (c) to face to
    (d) facing to

13. A: I haven't seen Daniel lately.
    B: He has been working at _____ since last Monday.

    (a) any west branch
    (b) west branch
    (c) the west branch
    (d) every west branch

14. A: We _____ for all the work we've done.
    B: You're right. I'll talk to the supervisor.

    (a) get paid
    (b) might be paid
    (c) must have been paid
    (d) should get paid

15. A: Kenneth is an excellent architect. I love his work.
    B: Well, he's not _____ architect as he used to be.

    (a) as great an
    (b) as a great
    (c) such great an
    (d) a such great

16. A: When do you think Frank will be back?
    B: He'll be here _____ you get home.

    (a) the time by
    (b) by this time
    (c) this time by
    (d) by the time

17. A: Where did the accident take place?

    B: It occurred _____ the corner of Travis Hill Drive and 23rd Avenue.

(a) for
(b) from
(c) at
(d) to

18. A: My mom is from Santiago, Chile.

    B: _____! I used to work there.

(a) What a coincidence
(b) What coincidence
(c) How coincidence
(d) How a coincidence

19. A: Can you make a cake for Jose's birthday?

    B: I don't think I _____. I have too much work to do.

(a) am
(b) will be
(c) will be able to
(d) could do

20. A: Which color _____ prefer for the book cover?

    B: Why don't you ask him?

(a) do you suppose Jeffrey would
(b) does Jeffrey suppose to
(c) is Jeffrey would suppose to
(d) you suppose Jeffrey to

Part II **Questions 21—40**

Choose the best answer for the blank.

---

21. As people live longer, it is suggested that having hobbies is all _____ individuals will have more years to live after retirement than they used to.

(a) as important as
(b) most important because
(c) more important
(d) the more important because

22. Humans differ from all other creatures _____ they have a sophisticated way of communication called language.

(a) given that
(b) in that
(c) such that
(d) provided that

23. When she bought those stocks a decade ago, they weren't worth _____.

(a) everything
(b) nothing
(c) anything
(d) something

24. After searching for a job for six months, Kimberly finally found _____ in Memphis.

(a) it
(b) one
(c) thing
(d) another

25. The managers who attended the
    seminar _____ all satisfied.

    (a) is
    (b) was
    (c) are
    (d) were

26. I had no choice but to watch that
    movie because every other one
    was sold out, but it turned out to be
    _____.

    (a) good quite a movie
    (b) good a movie quite
    (c) quite a good movie
    (d) quite good a movie

27. Experts believe _____ because
    of a cataclysmic event 65 million
    years ago.

    (a) it highly likely that dinosaurs
        became extinct
    (b) dinosaurs be highly likely to
        become extinct
    (c) highly likely for dinosaurs to
        become extinct
    (d) highly likely that dinosaurs
        became extinct

28. One _____ food before
    the advent of refrigeration was
    marinating.

    (a) of the methods used to preserve
    (b) of the method used to preserve
    (c) of the methods is used to
        preserving
    (d) of the method is used to preserve

29. Over the past 10 years, the average
    annual tuition has increased about 8
    percent _____ year.

    (a) another
    (b) some
    (c) the
    (d) a

30. The lecture is part of a series on
    alternative energy sources _____
    will replace fossil fuels in the future.

    (a) which
    (b) who
    (c) whose
    (d) whatever

31. _____ the server sooner, we
    would not be in such trouble now.

    (a) We replaced so
    (b) Had we replaced
    (c) Have we replaced so
    (d) replaced we so

32. The few members able to attend last
    week's fundraiser _____ all
    from other countries.

    (a) is
    (b) are
    (c) was
    (d) were

33. Activists highlight the dangers
    facing popular animals like bears
    _____ public concern for the
    environment.

    (a) of a means creating as
    (b) creating as a means of
    (c) a means of creating as
    (d) as a means of creating

34. You'd better check out what the fastest way is _____ to a foreign country.

    (a) having delivered a package
    (b) to have delivered a package
    (c) having a package delivered
    (d) to have a package delivered

35. The number of different channels available on TVs these days _____.

    (a) can be overwhelmed
    (b) can be overwhelming
    (c) are to overwhelm
    (d) overwhelm themselves

36. _____ into the living room when I heard a thump outside.

    (a) No sooner had I stepped
    (b) No sooner I did stepped
    (c) Did I no sooner stepped
    (d) Had I no sooner stepped

37. Only if it is done this way _____.

    (a) it will be possible
    (b) will it be possible
    (c) it is possible
    (d) has been it possible

38. I will let you know as soon as it _____.

    (a) had arrived
    (b) did arrive
    (c) arrived
    (d) arrives

39. Mr. Perez was considered the best person to represent the district, so they decided _____.

    (a) to appoint him as a delegate
    (b) appointing him as a delegate
    (c) appointing for him as a delegate
    (d) to appoint for him as a delegate

40. It is believed _____ the standard of care for diabetics.

    (a) the new test becoming
    (b) that the new test will become
    (c) whether the new test will become
    (d) for the new test to become

Identify the option that contains an awkward expression or an error in grammar.

41. (a) A: I had never seen a forest fire before. It wasn't at all like I expected.
    (b) B: Me, neither! It was horrifying!
    (c) A: What freaked me out the most were the smoke.
    (d) B: I know. The forest kept smoldering for hours after the fire put out.

42. (a) A: How a gorgeous painting! It is really stunning.
    (b) B: Yes, it has been popular at this exhibition.
    (c) A: Do you know who painted it?
    (d) B: Yeah, this is one of Picasso's early paintings.

43. (a) A: You're running late this morning.
    (b) B: My car won't start. Could you give me a ride to work?
    (c) A: I don't have time but you can borrow my bike if you want.
    (d) B: No, thanks. I'd rather to take the subway.

44. (a) A: Meg, would you like a slice of peach pie?
    (b) B: No, thanks. I think I'll pass.
    (c) A: You don't care for dessert? Or is it what you're cutting down on sugar?
    (d) B: Neither. I just feel stuffed after such a big dinner.

45. (a) A: I can't believe I am going to the Maldives on Friday.
    (b) B: Remember packing some sunscreen and a bathing suit.
    (c) A: I am thinking of buying all that there, actually.
    (d) B: Suit yourself. But if I were you, I'd take care of it before you leave.

Part IV Questions 46—50

Identify the option that contains an awkward expression or an error in grammar.

46. (a) The Sunoco Hotel in San Jose is celebrating its 20th anniversary. (b) From June 15 to July 15, guests can enjoy a one-night stay in a single suite for just $150. (c) Guests who reserve a suite for the evening of July 15 will be treated to complimentary bottle of champagne and a fruit basket. (d) All guests who visit the hotel during the event will also receive a free breakfast.

47. (a) Sleep deprivation is becoming a very serious issue. (b) Parents with young children are familiar with the difficulty of getting enough sleep but many others suffer from a constant lack of sleep, too. (c) Many different things can be affected people's ability to get a good night's sleep. (d) These include caffeine, stress, and/ or a lack of exercise.

48. (a) Are you looking to find a great name for your company? (b) For many companies, the task of branding can be challenging, that is why at Sunnyside Communications we like to do the hard work for you. (c) The first thing to do is have a brief meeting. (d) This is an opportunity for you to learn about the services we offer, and for us to better understand what your company is all about.

49. (a) Throughout human history, honey has been one of the most valuable of nature's gifts. (b) But the value of this sweet wonder hasn't been just for the taste buds. (c) For centuries, honey has been known as its healing powers. (d) Cleopatra used it as part of her daily beauty routine because honey naturally attracts and keeps moisture.

50. (a) A so-called smartphone offers more sophisticated computing ability than a basic cell phone. (b) Regular cell phones can run simple applications based on general platforms like Java Q. (c) By contrast, the user is allowed to install and run far more advanced applications with a smartphone. (d) Demand for advanced mobile devices with robust processors and bigger memory had been growing fast for the last several years.

This is the end of the Grammar section. Do NOT move on to the next section until instructed to do so. You are NOT allowed to turn to any other section of the test.

VOCABULARY

DIRECTIONS

This part of the exam tests your vocabulary skills. You will have 15 minutes to complete the 50 questions. Be sure to follow the directions given by the proctor.

Part I **Questions 1—25**

Choose the best answer for the blank.

1. A: Let's have a coffee break.
    B: I was about to _____ the same thing.

    (a) admit
    (b) suggest
    (c) appeal
    (d) speak

2. A: I have to go now. Catch you later.
    B: Okay. _____ .

    (a) Cool down
    (b) Take care
    (c) Chin up
    (d) Chill out

3. A: Would you like to go to a movie tonight?
    B: It depends on what is _____ .

    (a) running
    (b) catching
    (c) watching
    (d) playing

4. A: I hate doing the laundry.
    B: I didn't know it was a _____ to you.

    (a) load
    (b) burden
    (c) cargo
    (d) freight

5. A: Your bike looks a lot cooler since the last time I saw it!
    B: Thanks. I've put a lot of _____ into fixing it up.

    (a) cost
    (b) effort
    (c) pain
    (d) struggle

6. A: You have always been late when submitting reports.
    B: I'll try to be _____ with my time management in the future.

    (a) slower
    (b) sooner
    (c) longer
    (d) better

7. A: Chinese is so difficult!
    B: Every language is _____ at first, but it only gets easier.

    (a) frustrating
    (b) embarrassing
    (c) exhilarating
    (d) raving

8. A: Singapore has become an economic _____ .
    B: Right. It's small but very strong.

    (a) sucker
    (b) titan
    (c) hazard
    (d) dope

9. A: This ATM isn't working!
   B: You might have entered your PIN
   _____.

   (a) inconceivably
   (b) incorrectly
   (c) immediately
   (d) incorrigibly

10. A: Why don't you wait until Derek
    arrives?
    B: Sorry, but I have a plane to
    _____.

    (a) catch
    (b) drive
    (c) ride
    (d) pull

11. A: I can't believe I got the
    scholarship!
    B: It would appear all your hard work
    finally _____.

    (a) worked out
    (b) paid off
    (c) kicked off
    (d) ended up

12. A: Is that you, Barbara? What a small
    world!
    B: I didn't expect to _____ you
    here at Greg's party.

    (a) glance
    (b) peep
    (c) see
    (d) bump

13. A: Do you know what your picture is
    worth?
    B: Actually, I've never had it
    _____.

    (a) perceived
    (b) reverted
    (c) appraised
    (d) measured

14. A: Don't you think the construction
    site is too loud?
    B: Yeah, the noise is just _____.

    (a) unbearable
    (b) unanimous
    (c) unyielding
    (d) unscathed

15. A: This bookshelf doesn't look very
    well made.
    B: It might look that way, but it's
    actually quite _____.

    (a) hefty
    (b) racy
    (c) proxy
    (d) sturdy

16. A: I'm sorry about the awful things
    I said last night.
    B: Don't worry about it. Let's just
    bury the _____.

    (a) sword
    (b) grudge
    (c) baggage
    (d) hatchet

17. A: How about going for a walk to the lake?

    B: I'd love to go out for a _____.

    (a) stroll
    (b) picnic
    (c) trip
    (d) race

18. A: Let me buy you lunch.

    B: No, let's _____ the bill.

    (a) split
    (b) pick
    (c) pay
    (d) send

19. A: Did you look at Marisa's proposal? It's just too shoddy.

    B: Yeah, it leaves a lot to be _____.

    (a) pampered
    (b) understood
    (c) desired
    (d) fixed

20. A: Roger, did you choose a restaurant?

    B: Not yet. I can't make up my _____.

    (a) decision
    (b) mind
    (c) question
    (d) choice

21. A: Your proposal was excellent!

    B: Thanks. I thought there were some issues to be _____.

    (a) raised
    (b) dragged
    (c) opened
    (d) taken

22. A: The deadline is unreasonable, isn't it?

    B: Yeah, there's no _____ for error.

    (a) extra
    (b) tolerance
    (c) room
    (d) contemplation

23. A: You're not allowed to park there.

    B: Really? But Mrs. Lewis _____ me that I would be able to.

    (a) misled
    (b) assured
    (c) meddled
    (d) considered

24. A: What happened? Someone must be held _____ for the damages incurred.

    B: I don't know. I just got here myself.

    (a) accountable
    (b) responsive
    (c) blamed
    (d) guilty

25. A: How are you getting along?

    B: Same as _____.

    (a) average
    (b) general
    (c) usual
    (d) ordinary

Part II   **Questions 26—50**

Choose the best answer for the blank.

26. Many experts criticize the current welfare programs and argue that they should be _____ .

   (a) renovated
   (b) renewed
   (c) reformed
   (d) remodeled

27. With our teaching method, students can learn to _____ words in a foreign language as well as a native speaker.

   (a) announce
   (b) espouse
   (c) declare
   (d) pronounce

28. If you think you are a victim of sexual harassment, do not hesitate to _____ an official complaint to our board.

   (a) file
   (b) stir
   (c) harbor
   (d) advance

29. The new marketing manager agreed to try advertising on the Internet to _____ sales.

   (a) extend
   (b) reduce
   (c) rise
   (d) boost

30. Healthy brain development is a critical factor in determining _____ skills.

   (a) sensitive
   (b) cognitive
   (c) positive
   (d) mandatory

31. Lion prides usually _____ of up to 15 females and cubs, and one or two males accompanying them.

   (a) consist
   (b) equate
   (c) comprise
   (d) compose

32. Residents have employed a new technology to _____ rainwater to use for gardening purposes during times of dry weather.

   (a) detain
   (b) sustain
   (c) retain
   (d) contain

33. Until recently, researchers believed that babies are, even when they are in the same room, _____ of each other's presence.

   (a) abusive
   (b) oblivious
   (c) magnanimous
   (d) vulnerable

34. Charles Garcia, one of the most famous pianists in the world, is _____ for his impeccable technique, stylistic versatility, and expression.

    (a) esteemed
    (b) derived
    (c) fulfilled
    (d) amassed

35. _____ to poor economic conditions, the job market is becoming more competitive.

    (a) According
    (b) Apt
    (c) Due
    (d) Next

36. Aboriginals who arrived in Australia about 60,000 years ago were the first _____ of the continent.

    (a) inhabitants
    (b) residents
    (c) inmates
    (d) tenants

37. There is conclusive evidence that most of the global warming that has taken place over the past five decades is _____ to human activities.

    (a) attributable
    (b) applicable
    (c) disposable
    (d) disputable

38. As Shirley had been ill for a month and missed many classes, she was _____ from final exams.

    (a) exempt
    (b) sanctioned
    (c) prevented
    (d) scrutinized

39. The police _____ every passenger who passed through the gate based on a report that someone was smuggling drugs.

    (a) swindled
    (b) confiscated
    (c) balked
    (d) frisked

40. The transportation workers' union went on strike in a show of _____ with the fired bus drivers.

    (a) equity
    (b) opportunity
    (c) solidarity
    (d) consensus

41. Religious groups often consider natural wonders like the Himalayas as _____.

    (a) vain
    (b) scanty
    (c) sacred
    (d) gaudy

42. Some companies are willing to do anything to _____ the law and dodge taxes.

    (a) observe
    (b) enact
    (c) skirt
    (d) enforce

43. The old man's health has deteriorated so much that it seems almost meaningless to _____ the cause.

    (a) amplify
    (b) depict
    (c) deny
    (d) pinpoint

44. Although he doesn't make a lot of money, he believes that what he is doing is worthwhile and _____ for something.

    (a) counts
    (b) adds
    (c) values
    (d) benefits

45. Martin Luther King, Jr. opposed the _____ of blacks and whites in schools.

    (a) segregation
    (b) segmentation
    (c) scrutiny
    (d) simplification

46. If a cat shows its belly to other cats, it _____ a surrender and the fight is over.

    (a) signifies
    (b) professes
    (c) illuminates
    (d) illustrates

47. It was truly amazing how Diane remained _____ and calm in the midst of such political turmoil.

    (a) piqued
    (b) poised
    (c) outgoing
    (d) restive

48. The actress was devastated when she found _____ comments written about her on the Internet.

    (a) bereaving
    (b) disparaging
    (c) impeaching
    (d) construing

49. The government _____ the marshlands near Mt. Allison and placed them under the authority of the Parks and Recreation Department.

    (a) bolstered
    (b) restored
    (c) reclaimed
    (d) refurbished

50. HML _____ its partnership with TLC Communications in the wake of the recent financial scandal.

    (a) liquidated
    (b) liquefied
    (c) bankrupted
    (d) resolved

This is the end of the Vocabulary section. Do NOT move on to the Reading Comprehension section until instructed to do so. You are NOT allowed to turn to any other section of the test.

READING
COMPREHENSION

Part I **Questions 1—16**

Read the passage. Then choose the option that best completes the passage.

1. *The Cove* won an Academy Award for Best Documentary Film in 2010. The film is about the violent killing of dolphins. This takes place in a national park in Japan by men with spears and knives. Western audiences were horrified by the brutal killing. The film had some excellent camera work. The documentary received mixed reviews from Japanese audiences. Some were shocked to learn about the killings. Japanese people were even more surprised to learn that some of the dolphin meat was fed to Japanese school children. Critics of the film

_____.

(a) were impressed by the documentary's style
(b) encouraged protests against the killings
(c) refused to watch previews of the film
(d) described it as biased and misleading

2.
Dear Anna Hugo,

Congratulations! You have been selected for the Wagner Opera Camp. You will join the 2011 summer session. There is a long waiting list of eager applicants. Please confirm your attendance by April 15. If you do wish to attend, fill out the enclosed registration materials. Then send them to us, along with a check for $595 to cover your room and board. We _____ this special opportunity. This is your chance to be trained by masters in the field of opera. Thank you.

Ned Winston
Awards and Financial Aid Department

(a) want to drop the fees for
(b) encourage you to apply for
(c) appreciate your participation in
(d) hope you will take advantage of

3. A new study now shows that human growth hormone can indeed enhance performance. Researchers in Australia said the hormone benefited athletes in sprint events. This is true especially when a split second can decide the winner, as in running or swimming. A total of 103 male and female athletes were tested over the course of two months. They received injections of either growth hormone or salt water. The hormone improved sprinting on a bicycle by 4 percent. This proves that human growth hormone _____.

    (a) needs to be further tested
    (b) boosts athletic performance
    (c) should be banned from all sporting events
    (d) destroys athletic performance in the long run

4. Jeannette Walls is the author of the book *The Glass Castle*. It is a true story based on her own life. She writes about how she _____. Her father was an alcoholic. Her mother was like a child. She could not feed or take care of Jeannette and her brothers and sisters. There was rarely any food in the house. Jeannette knew she had to get away from her parents. She escaped to New York. She began working for a newspaper there and wrote her book.

    (a) always wanted to be a writer
    (b) spent her early life in poverty
    (c) taught herself to read and write
    (d) helped her parents to earn bread

5. The German chemist August Kekule is considered to be one of the founders of modern organic chemistry. In 1858 he showed that carbon can link with itself to form long chains. For several years afterward, he worked on another problem: determining the shape of a benzene molecule. One day in 1965, he had a nap. The scientist had a dream of a snake biting its own tail. That was his answer. The structure was a ring. This story shows that _____.

    (a) triumph is built on the failures of others
    (b) luck usually follows a long period of training
    (c) even achievement is 1% inspiration and 99% work
    (d) success can come suddenly and when least expected

6. The Masai Mara National Reserve is the most famous reserve in East Africa. It is unfenced and next to the Serengeti National Park. This allows the wildlife to roam freely between Kenya and Tanzania in search of food. The best time to visit is during the dry season, from July to March. Tall grasses can hide animals in the wet season. _____, it is much easier to view the animals. While there, you can view wildlife such as lions, leopards, and hyenas.

    (a) When the grasses are low to the ground
    (b) As the sun starts to rise over the horizon
    (c) In the time when most tourists stay away
    (d) During the period when the weather gets cooler

7.

Dear Editor,

I'm writing in response to the article "Child Labor in the Developing World," published on October 18. The problem is not the evil factory owners but it is consumers like you and me. We are always trying to save money but we need to stop and ask ourselves how it is possible to make something so cheaply. Chances are that it was made by child laborers, as many cheap articles of clothing come from India and China. Child labor and child slavery are common in these countries. We must stop buying cheap clothing made in these places. We might be helping a system that _____.

    (a) makes clothing expensive
    (b) produces attractive items
    (c) provides jobs to people
    (d) uses children as slaves

8. More and more people in the West are turning towards acupuncture. It has become a way to treat allergies and other health problems. Many say that acupuncture makes them feel refreshed and renewed afterwards. Some even believe this method should _____. However, it might be dangerous to stop seeing doctors altogether. Acupuncture cannot cure everything. People should learn as much as they can about both Eastern and Western medicine. Then they can choose the method that is best to improve their condition.

    (a) be covered by insurance companies
    (b) be made more readily available
    (c) replace Western medicine
    (d) come with warning labels

9. People are always trying to find ways to lose weight. Scientists in California may have found a secret ingredient that helps dieters lose weight. A chemical found in peppers was shown to boost energy burning in bodies. In an experiment, those who were given high doses of this chemical burned more body fat than people who had been given pills that did nothing. The researchers believe that the pepper chemical works by attaching itself to another type of receptor. This receptor helps signal to the brain and then starts a process that _____.

(a) causes the body to burn calories
(b) increases the temperature of cells
(c) decreases a person's desire to eat food
(d) makes the brain release more chemicals

10. Cats innately scratch objects in their environment for normal reasons. One is to remove the dead outer layer of their claws. Another is to mark their territory by leaving the scent from the glands on their paws. Scratching also leaves a visual mark to let others know they were there. Cats may also have extra energy and need to work it off by scratching. Because scratching is normal behavior, _____. Instead, try to resolve scratching problems by redirecting the scratching onto acceptable objects.

(a) owners might consider declawing their cats
(b) scolding the cat is an effective way to stop it
(c) cats will leave their scent on household items
(d) you should not try to prevent them from scratching

11. Knitting with cotton is _____. Wool is popular among knitters because it is easy to work with. However, some people are allergic to it. In that case, cotton is a good replacement. Cotton is especially good for light clothing. Unlike wool, cotton can be washed in a washing machine. Cotton is often used for summer clothing. It is great for those with sensitive skin as well. Cotton yarn is less expensive than wool yarn. It holds together well and gets softer as time passes.

(a) much better for younger people
(b) different from knitting with wool
(c) excellent for your fingers and hands
(d) simple and often preferred to other fabrics

12. Martin Luther King, Jr., was a great man. He helped improve civil rights in the U.S. He believed that all people are created equally. King grew up in the South, where he experienced racism. He wanted to change the system so that he and others like him could have fair treatment. However, he was against violence. Instead, he used peaceful methods to work for change. He won the Nobel Peace Prize in 1964. King was inspired by the teachings of Mahatma Gandhi, who

_____.

   (a) damaged his health by going on hunger strikes
   (b) fought for change with different methods
   (c) shared his belief in non-violence
   (d) found his work too elementary

13. Artists use different styles in their paintings and drawings. Before the abstract movement, artists showed only things that were able to be recognized. These were things like people, animals, or places. Abstract artists did not follow this style. Rather, they used color and shape in their paintings to show emotions. Indeed, the viewer may not see any specific objects. It is not painted to look like something specific. This means an abstract painting _____.
Jackson Pollock is an example of an abstract artist. He dripped and tossed paint onto canvases in what appeared to be random patterns.

   (a) is a better representation of an object
   (b) will show exactly what an object looks like
   (c) is done with methods similar to traditional art
   (d) will sometimes look nothing like what exists in nature

14. The application period for renewing vehicle registrations has been extended. You will now have until June 30. Fees _____. The fee for a standard sedan is $20.00, for a trailer is $35.00, and for an off-road vehicle is $35.00. Commercial vehicles are weighed. The fees are then based on weight. Before you can renew your registration, the vehicle must be insured. When driving, you must carry the pink insurance card for that vehicle. If you are caught without the card, you will be fined.

   (a) change depending on what day it is entered into the system
   (b) depend on how old the vehicle being registered is
   (c) differ according to the brand and model of the car
   (d) vary by the type and weight of the vehicle

15.

> Dear Margaret,
>
> Thank you very much for your invitation. I wish we could spend Memorial Day weekend with you in the Hamptons. _____, my wife Eliza has just undergone surgery. She had her hip replaced. Therefore, she cannot leave the house for the next four weeks. She is healing well, but needs help around the house. Insurance will not pay for a nurse and I am the only person who can help her. I'm sure you understand. We'll miss spending the holiday with you, but I'm sure we'll have more chances in the future.
>
> Sincerely,
> Howard

(a) Incredibly
(b) Foreseeably
(c) Unfortunately
(d) Coincidentally

16. The World Wildlife Fund for Nature (WWF) is an international organization. It is devoted to protecting the environment. It focuses on saving animals. Its goals are to be admired. Yet it has been in some trouble. _____, in June 2009, it had a fight with an organization in Cambodia. The WWF claimed the Mekong dolphin was being killed by pollution. In fact, most dolphins died from fishing-related accidents. A local person said the WWF made up numbers to raise money from donors.

(a) For example
(b) Regardless
(c) In addition
(d) Above all

Read the passage and the question. Then choose the option that best answers the question.

17. Movies can be powerful. They can change the way people think and feel. That is why Thai filmmaker Rutt Jumpamule made his movie. It is a touching animation called *Sunset Love Song*. He made the film after his friend's brother killed himself. Jumpamule said he wanted his movie to give advice to viewers. He wanted to help other people like his friend. *Sunset Love Song* is about a boy and girl who live in Bangkok. They feel lonely and are going through some tough times. It sounds simple but the movie has a deeper message.

Q: What is the passage mainly about?
(a) The suicide of a friend's brother
(b) One man's artistic product
(c) The power of movies
(d) Living in Bangkok

18. On April 20, 2010, a drilling rig exploded and eleven workers went missing. The rig then collapsed, creating a major oil spill in the Gulf of Mexico. The oil is terrible for the water and wildlife so people could not fish in that area for quite some time. The state of Louisiana has been most affected by this oil spill. The company responsible is BP, an energy corporation, and will have to pay billions of dollars to clean up the mess. During a visit to the Gulf Coast, President Barack Obama promised to use his power to help the situation.

Q: What is the passage mainly about?
(a) A President's pledge to assist an area
(b) Cleaning up in a poor part of the country
(c) An oil spill caused by an energy company
(d) A natural disaster that has devastated residents

19. Vegetables are good for you, but they can also make you sick. Sometimes raw vegetables like spinach and lettuce have bacteria on them. It could be because the farming water was unsafe. Or it could be because the people who handled them did not wash their hands. Some bacteria, such as E. coli, can be deadly. It is wise to buy produce from responsible vendors. You could also cook the vegetables to kill the bacteria. However, salad items like lettuce do not taste good when cooked.

Q: What is the main idea of the passage?
(a) You must be careful with certain produce.
(b) Vegetables are not that good for you.
(c) Vegetables have to be cooked.
(d) Bacteria can be dangerous.

20. Roy C. Sullivan was a ranger working in a U.S. Park. In 1942, lightning struck his leg. Thirty years later, he was standing in the office at the ranger station. Lightning struck him again and set his hair on fire. The lightning strikes continued to happen. Lightning would strike him again and again, for a total of seven times. He is the only person to have been hit by lightning this many times. Scientists say that his work as a ranger put him more at risk.

Q: What is the passage mainly about?
(a) The chances of being struck by lightning
(b) Where lightning is most likely to strike
(c) One man's unique experience
(d) Dangerous forms of work

21. Roy Pearson, a judge in Washington, D.C., went to the dry cleaners to pick up a suit he had cleaned. However, he discovered that the pants did not match his jacket, and he became very angry. The dry cleaners found the matching pants several days later yet Pearson denied they were his pants. He demanded that the cleaners pay him $1,000, the full price of the suit, but they insisted that the pants were his and refused to pay him the money. Pearson sued them for $65 million.

Q: What is the best title for the news report?
(a) Angry Lawyer Takes Legal Action
(b) Judge Takes Cleaners to Court
(c) Pants Do Not Match Jacket
(d) Dry Cleaners Win Lawsuit

22. Some people know of Bosnia from the Bosnian War (1992-1995). The country, now known as Bosnia and Herzegovina, is shedding its sad past. It is becoming a popular travel destination. Those who love outdoor activities will enjoy hiking in the mountains. Visitors more interested in culture can examine the old castles and art. More and more couples are choosing to go there on their honeymoons. Some may want to learn more about the war. They can visit parks and sites created for victims of the war.

Q: What is the passage mainly about?
(a) The effects of the Bosnian War
(b) Tourism in Bosnia and Herzegovina
(c) The history of Bosnia and Herzegovina
(d) Unique cultural traits of Bosnia and Herzegovina

23. Braces help straighten teeth by putting steady pressure on your teeth. Springs or rubber bands can be used to move teeth in a specific direction. The pressure causes the tooth to loosen from the gums. When the tooth stops moving, the bone grows in to provide support to the tooth in its new place. This movement should be gradual. Otherwise, the patient risks losing teeth. By wearing braces over time, teeth are moved into their proper position. Most people wear braces for two to three years.

Q: What may happen if the braces move teeth too quickly?
(a) Teeth will fall out.
(b) The braces will break.
(c) The rubber bands will snap.
(d) Teeth will straighten faster.

24. The sun causes water to evaporate. The water changes from liquid to gas and rises up. These gases cool and later form clouds in the sky. This process is called condensation. When clouds become too heavy, the water falls back down to the ground. This can be in the form of snow or rain. The water will then evaporate again. It is a continuous movement of water on, above, and below the surface of the Earth. The entire process is called the water cycle.

Q: Which is correct according to the passage?
(a) The sun is responsible for life on Earth.
(b) Condensation occurs very quickly.
(c) Water is heaviest in liquid form.
(d) The water cycle never stops.

25. Electronics such as laptops, smartphones and e-book readers, may be causing people to lose sleep. They shine bright light into our eyes right before we go to bed. Scientists think they may trick our brains. They make the brain think it's daytime. This might cause sleeping problems. E-book readers like the iPad shine light directly into the reader's eyes. It does it at a distance that is closer than watching TV. Scientists recommend reading regular books instead because they help relax people.

Q: Why are people losing sleep according to the passage?
(a) They are not reading traditional books.
(b) They are exposed to too much light.
(c) Their eyes cannot adjust to the light.
(d) Electronics are fooling their brains.

26. Do you use a digital camera? Why not make a beautiful photo book from those images? With Snapfrog, it is easy to save and display your favorite pictures. Simply choose the files you want in the book. We will take care of the rest. This includes laying out the photos and binding the pages. At the end you'll get a professional book of photos. Photo books make great gifts. Create a photo book and save 30% on additional copies for family and friends.

Q: Which is correct according to the ad?
(a) All photo books are 30% off.
(b) Snapfrog will design the photo book.
(c) Customers must send prints of their photos.
(d) Family members will get a discount on their books.

27. In 1989, more than 1 million people protested in Beijing. They wanted more freedom from the government. The protests were mostly peaceful. However, the Chinese government did not approve. Protestors were arrested and some were beaten. On June 4, the Chinese army sent tanks to the protest site. They arrested 10,000 people and killed thousands. Countries around the world were horrified by what happened. The United States stopped selling arms to China. It also punished China by denying trade and help for development.

Q: Why did the United States stop trading with China?
(a) To deny help for the protestors
(b) To weaken the Chinese military
(c) To send a message of disapproval
(d) To protest China's high capital punishment

28. The Wampanoag tribe is a Native American tribe. They lived in the Northeast of the United States. The tribe roamed the area and set up villages. That was in the early 1600s, before many Europeans settled in America. The Wampanoag farmed when they could. They also fished for food. The people started to die when Europeans arrived in 1614. The Europeans brought new diseases. The Wampanoag were not used to these germs. By 1620, 5,000 Wampanoag people remained. Over half of them had been killed by disease.

Q: Which is correct according to the passage?
(a) There used to be more than 10,000 Wampanoag people in the U.S.
(b) The European settlers took away land from the Wampanoag.
(c) The Europeans set out to kill many Wampanoag people.
(d) The Wampanoag no longer exist in the United States.

29.

Dear Ms. Milton,

Ticket prices have remained the same for the last 10 years. But our rent has been increasing. Therefore, we must raise the price of our season tickets from $258 to $295. Single viewing tickets will have a price increase, too. We hope that you will buy season tickets next year despite this change. The Vartan Ballet relies on season ticket holders. They fill 30% of the seating at each performance. Without your support we would not exist. To purchase tickets please visit us at www. vartanballet.ca. We look forward to having you in our audience again next year.

Q: Which is correct according to the letter?
(a) Only 30% of the seats are filled at each performance.
(b) The Vartan Ballet has been losing money each year.
(c) Season tickets were $258 for the last decade.
(d) Ms. Milton does not like the ballet.

30. A star is made of gases. As its gases burn, they give off light and heat. When the gas runs out, the star stops burning and begins to die. As the star cools, the outer layers of the star pull in toward the middle. The star becomes smaller and smaller. The space resulting from the dead star is a black hole. Think of the Earth being made into the size of a marble. That is how tightly this black hole is packed. Gravity pulls the star in toward its center.

Q: Which is correct according to the passage?
(a) The Earth can become a black hole.
(b) Stars repel gravity as they die.
(c) A black hole has no light.
(d) Living stars have gases.

31. Chimpanzees are intelligent animals. Some chimps can even do better than humans in some memory tasks. One study flashed the numbers 1 to 9 on a touchscreen. They appeared in random areas on the screen. The chimps had to memorize the locations of the numbers. They then had to press the correct square to recall the numbers in order. They were able to do this better than some humans. Scientists say it is because humans made a trade off during evolution. To gain certain capabilities, we had to lose other ones.

Q: Which is correct according to the passage?
(a) The use of hands is what distinguishes humans.
(b) Humans will always perform better than animals.
(c) Chimps do not have all the capabilities of humans.
(d) Animals in the wild are less intelligent than those in labs.

32. The praying mantis is an unusual-looking insect. There are 2,000 species in the praying mantis family. They range in size from half an inch to over six inches. They stalk and catch live prey, usually other insects. However, they also eat lizards, snakes, frogs, birds, and rodents. They are also cannibals; sometimes a female praying mantis will eat the male after mating. The praying mantis is closely related to termites. But the praying mantis is not usually thought of as a pest.

Q: What is correct according to the passage?
(a) The praying mantis will sometimes eat its young.
(b) Termites are considered to be pests to humans.
(c) Other insects also prey on the praying mantis.
(d) The praying mantis has no known enemies.

33. Louisa May Alcott is the author of many books, her most famous being *Little Women*, published in 1868. It is a story about four sisters in the 19th century and the difficulties for women growing up in that time. Alcott was born in 1832, a time when women did not enjoy equal rights. Alcott never married because she wanted to remain free. She continued to write books. Like other authors, she used her writing to change the way people think.

Q: What can be inferred from the passage?
(a) Married women lacked certain freedoms.
(b) Alcott never dated any men in her lifetime.
(c) *Little Women* was a popular book in the 1800s.
(d) Alcott wanted equal rights for whites and blacks.

34. Hurricanes are a type of tropical storm. They have fierce winds of over 75 miles per hour. A hurricane begins as a thunderstorm over warm areas of the ocean. It picks up power from the warmth and moisture. It will then weaken over areas with cooler water temperatures. A hurricane can also create a tornado. A tornado is a column of wind. It is formed by twisting air. That is why a tornado is sometimes called a twister. Tornadoes destroy homes and property. They cause damage and can kill people.

Q: What can be inferred from the passage?
(a) Hurricanes lose power as temperatures drop.
(b) Tornadoes kill more people than hurricanes.
(c) Hurricanes travel faster than tornadoes.
(d) Tornadoes bring wind and rain to areas.

35. Pueblo pottery is very different from other types of clay art. It does not use any machinery. Other types of pottery may use a potter's wheel. This is a machine that creates vases and round objects. Pueblo potters roll the clay into long pieces by hand. Then they coil the pieces into layers of circles. The lack of machinery means that each piece is unique. Its individuality is what makes it attractive to art collectors. For that reason, Pueblo pottery pieces make excellent gifts.

Q: Which is likely to follow in this passage?
(a) Some people who collect Pueblo art
(b) Examples of famous Pueblo potters
(c) Places to buy Pueblo pottery
(d) The history of Pueblo art

36. There is something unique about the owl's appearance that makes people think they are wise or powerful. Some cultures believe owls have magic powers but owls are no more magical than other birds. Their features help owls hunt, especially in the night. Their big, round heads turn 135 degrees in each direction and their large forward-facing eyes can focus on small creatures like mice. Their sharp beaks and claws help kill their prey. Owls also fly silently; therefore, their prey rarely hear them coming.

Q: What can be inferred from the passage?
(a) Most birds, including owls, build their nests in trees.
(b) While some birds make noise, owls are silent.
(c) Owls can turn their heads all the way around.
(d) Mice can be a source of food for owls.

37. Sometimes art fades, tears, or gets damaged. Professional restorers will try to make an artwork look like the original. However, restorers tend to influence the work, too. They might choose to remove a layer of paint or brighten colors. In doing so, they may change the art according to their tastes. Restorers use science to decide how to restore an artwork. Science can reveal the elements that make up a painting. However, scientists cannot make known the true intention of the artist. The best and safest approach would be to leave it alone.

Q: What can be inferred from the passage?
(a) The science behind restoration is complicated.
(b) The author is not a supporter of art restoration.
(c) Restoring is a field that requires years of study.
(d) Art restorers have backgrounds as artists themselves.

Part III **Questions 38 — 40**

Read the passage. Then identify the option that does NOT belong.

38. In response to numerous problems, the United States came out with a new $100 bill earlier this year. (a) The new and improved bill has been made to last up to seven years. (b) It features a security ribbon and a picture of a bell that changes colors. (c) People in the United States are spending less money these days due to the economic recession. (d) The changes were made to make it more difficult to make fake $100 bills.

39. A new law in the province of Ontario requires all school districts to offer classes online. (a) The law was designed in order to give families more options. (b) I once took an online class in English literature myself when I was in high school. (c) Residents of the province stated that they are very much in favor of this new form of education. (d) After various surveys, the Ontario program is considered to be better than that of other areas.

40. You probably have not heard of it but the Dhole is a type of wild dog in India that is very social. (a) This endangered animal lives and travels with other Dholes in packs of 8 to 12. (b) Typically, you will find that there are more males than females in each pack. (c) Unlike with other dog relatives, the pack gets along well and fighting is rare. (d) There are even reports of Dholes becoming violent and attacking humans.

This is the end of the Reading Comprehension section. Please remain seated until the proctor has instructed otherwise. You are NOT allowed to turn to any other section of the test.

Actual Test 1

1

W Hi, Mark. How are you?

M _____

(a) That's fine.
(b) Enough for me.
(c) I'm well, thanks.
(d) I think one is OK.

2

M Do you want to come to the beach?

W _____

(a) Sure, it can be.
(b) But we'll have fun.
(c) Let's go there instead.
(d) I'm afraid I'm too busy.

3

W I regret not seeing that movie.

M _____

(a) The movie was on.
(b) Turn it over again.
(c) It's not what I saw.
(d) We can watch it later.

4

M Is this the way to the mall?

W _____

(a) Either one should work.
(b) Sure you can. Follow me.
(c) That's right. It's up ahead.
(d) It will be around here soon.

5

W This book is great. I recommend it.

M _____

(a) I've already read it.
(b) I'm glad it was on top.
(c) I didn't see a book there.
(d) But I thought you liked it.

6

M Congratulations on passing the exam.

W _____

(a) I believe I can win.
(b) Thanks, I'm so happy.
(c) I did the exam as well.
(d) Good, I'm happy for you.

7

W The baggage check-in line is so long.

M _____

(a) I've packed my bags.
(b) Check this line of them.
(c) My flight was comfortable.
(d) We should have come earlier.

8

M The report you did was excellent.

W _____

(a) I tried hard to be.
(b) This copy is good, too.
(c) I appreciate the compliment.
(d) Everyone hoped that it would.

9

W Are we booked into this hotel?

M _____

(a) I went to see the hotel.
(b) I'm glad you enjoyed it.
(c) OK, this one is a good book.
(d) Yes, we're here for two nights.

10

M You upset me with what you said.

W _____

(a) I will speak louder.
(b) Sorry, I didn't mean it.
(c) That wasn't how I did it.
(d) I said it in a different way.

11

W How about coming for a bite to eat?

M _____

(a) Yes, I ate already.
(b) I think it's delicious.
(c) That one's not tasty, either.
(d) Absolutely, I'm really hungry.

12

M Be careful. There's ice on the sidewalk.

W _____

(a) It will be icy soon.
(b) I know, I nearly slipped.
(c) I walked part of the way.
(d) It's not the right direction.

13

W It's amazing we agree on so many things.

M _____

(a) I do that, too.
(b) OK, but I agreed.
(c) We really think alike.
(d) Keep those things together.

14

M What did you think about the homework we got?

W _____

(a) That was correct.
(b) It was rather boring.
(c) It is the most of it.
(d) I'm doing my homework.

15

W I'd like to make a doctor's appointment, please.

M _____

(a) Whenever you are ill.
(b) That time will be fine.
(c) Tomorrow morning is free.
(d) The doctor ran some tests.

16

M What flavor of ice cream do you want?
W I'd like chocolate mint, please.
M And what size would you like?
W _____

(a) I'm eating it here.
(b) I'll have a medium.
(c) This one should fit.
(d) I want that size, too.

17

W Is my carry-on bag too heavy?
M I'll just check it for you.
W I hope it's not over the weight limit.
M _____

(a) It's just under.
(b) Just take one bag.
(c) No, you'll need it.
(d) Yes, I'll check in.

18

W I'm feeling so tired.

M Why is that?

W I couldn't get to sleep easily last night.

M _____

(a) I fell asleep then.

(b) Well, it's been a busy day.

(c) Let me know if you're tired.

(d) Maybe you'll sleep better tonight.

19

M Do you sell camera filters?

W No, we don't stock those.

M Do you know who sells them around here?

W _____

(a) Wherever they are sold.

(b) I put them in aisle two.

(c) We have a red and blue one.

(d) I recommend you try downtown.

20

M Hello, it's Bob. I'm calling to speak to Geoff.

W Sorry, he's not here right now.

M Can you tell him I called?

W _____

(a) Thanks a lot, Geoff.

(b) OK, I'll let him know.

(c) Call back later, then.

(d) Yes, I told him you called.

21

W Should I buy this jacket?

M No, it looks too big for you.

W But I really like it.

M _____

(a) Pay by credit card.

(b) It needs to be larger.

(c) It will keep you warm.

(d) Look for one that's smaller.

22

M Waitress, is our food coming soon?

W It shouldn't take too much longer.

M But how long will it be?

W _____

(a) I should wait longer.

(b) I can take your order.

(c) I'll go and check for you.

(d) I'm not sure what time it is.

23

W Oh, no. I forgot my wallet!

M Really? You mean it's still at home?

W Yes, I'm sorry. We'll have to go back.

M _____

(a) It's my mistake.

(b) I'll do a U-turn.

(c) Look in the bedroom.

(d) We can buy a new wallet.

24

M Shall we go walking tonight?

W Yes, we need the exercise.

M How about an hour after dinner?

W _____

(a) It should be on time.

(b) I haven't had dinner yet.

(c) I think walking is better.

(d) That sounds like a good idea.

25

W I don't like this hamburger.

M Why? What's wrong with it?

W It's really greasy.

M _____

(a) I've had enough to eat.

(b) We should come back again.

(c) Mine is like that as well.

(d) I wouldn't mind a hamburger.

26

M Can you help me with my math?
W Sure, what's the problem?
M I'm stuck on a geometry question.
W _____

(a) Just do the math.
(b) Show me which one.
(c) It's according to the math.
(d) That's another good answer.

27

W How will we get into town?
M The airport has shuttle buses.
W Oh, then which number do we take?
M _____

(a) I'll have to ask.
(b) Pick a number out.
(c) Perhaps a bus will do.
(d) We'll go in on the shuttle.

28

M This soccer game is so exciting!
W Yeah, who do you think will win it?
M I bet the blue team will.
W _____

(a) Right. They're far behind.
(b) That could have been a goal.
(c) No way. I think they'll lose.
(d) But there can only be one winner.

29

W Don't stay indoors all day.
M I won't. I'm going out later.
W Oh, what are you going to do?
M _____

(a) I'll do that as well.
(b) I'm going bike riding.
(c) I thought I'd head out.
(d) I might clean the house.

30

M Thanks for giving me a lift home.
W It was no trouble at all.
M Well, see you at work tomorrow.
W _____

(a) Me, too. I'll be leaving soon.
(b) Sure, I'll be in pretty early.
(c) I can drive you home this time.
(d) It shouldn't be any more trouble.

31

M Hi, Amanda. Nice to see you.
W Oh, hi, Trevor. I heard you were ill.
M I was but I'm much better now.
W What did you have, the flu?
M Yeah, it was a bad one.
W Well, good to see it's over.

Q: What is the main idea of the conversation?
(a) The man caught the flu.
(b) The man is no longer ill.
(c) The woman worries about the flu.
(d) The woman is glad to see the man.

32

W I've got too much work to do.
M Did you ask the boss to reduce your workload?
W Yes. He said he would, but he hasn't yet.
M Maybe you should talk to him again.
W I guess so. I'm getting stressed.
M Yeah, I know what you mean.

Q: What is the conversation mainly about?
(a) Getting enough work to do.
(b) Talking with the boss at work.
(c) Being at work while under stress.
(d) Asking the boss to give less work.

33

M Excuse me. Where are the Humanities buildings?

W Oh, you're going in the wrong direction.

M Really? Which way should I go?

W It's this way and right across campus.

M Right to the other end?

W Yes, just follow this path.

Q: What is the main topic of the conversation?

(a) What Humanities building to go to.

(b) What course to take in Humanities.

(c) How far the Humanities buildings are.

(d) How to get to the Humanities buildings.

34

W You never help around the house.

M But I'm at work till late.

W Not on the weekends. You just sit around.

M That's my time for relaxing.

W Can't you help a little with house cleaning?

M Well, OK, but only on weekends.

Q: What is the woman doing in the conversation?

(a) Showing the man how to clean.

(b) Cleaning the house with the man.

(c) Telling the man to do housework.

(d) Explaining what she already cleaned.

35

M The weather's beautiful outside.

W It sure is. Let's go to the park.

M I'd like to, but a baseball game is on TV.

W Then will you go after that?

M Sure, but it'll be an hour from now.

W That's OK. I can wait.

Q: What is the main topic of the conversation?

(a) Playing baseball.

(b) Enjoying nice weather.

(c) Visiting the park later.

(d) Watching an important game.

36

W Oh, look out for that car!

M Wow! What a crazy driver!

W He nearly hit us.

M He cut right in front of us.

W One day he'll have an accident.

M At least it wasn't with us.

Q: What is the main topic of the conversation?

(a) A car passing by.

(b) A dangerous driver.

(c) A bad car accident.

(d) A man that is speeding.

37

M I've been so busy lately.

W Doing what, just studying?

M Right. I've got no time for anything else.

W It's the same with me.

M It's because I've got several assignments due.

W Yeah. Me, too.

Q: What is the conversation mainly about?

(a) Studying hard together.

(b) Helping to do an assignment.

(c) Finding time to study.

(d) Spending a lot of time studying.

38

W This report has many errors.

M Really? Are you sure?

W Yes, five calculation errors were on this page.

M I'm really sorry. I will redo it.

W And there were spelling mistakes, too.

M Sorry, I'll fix it right away.

Q: Which is correct about the report according to the conversation?

(a) It was done by the woman.

(b) It features no calculations.

(c) It contains several errors.

(d) It will be fixed next month.

39

M Why were you late getting here?

W The bus got stuck in traffic.

M But you should have taken the subway.

W I know. I forgot the roads would be busy.

M Well, there is still time to catch a movie.

W Good. Let's get our tickets.

Q: Which is correct according to the conversation?

(a) The man had arrived late.

(b) The man recommended the subway.

(c) The woman just got off the subway.

(d) The woman cannot go to see a movie.

40

W Good morning, sir. Welcome to Korea.

M Thank you. Glad to be here.

W May I see your passport?

M Here you go. This is my first time in Korea.

W Are you here for business?

M No, just for a holiday.

Q: Which is correct about the man according to the conversation?

(a) He is departing from Korea.

(b) He could not find his passport.

(c) He has not been to Korea before.

(d) He traveled to Korea on business.

41

M Would you like to order now?

W Yes, I'll have the pizza, please.

M And would you like anything else?

W I think a small salad would be good.

M Anything to drink?

W Just some orange juice.

Q: Which is correct about the woman according to the conversation?

(a) She already ordered a meal.

(b) She does not want any pizza.

(c) She would like a salad dish.

(d) She wants water with her meal.

42

W I'm vacationing in New York this spring.

M Wow! I wish I could. I've never been there.

W Why don't you go sometime?

M I can't get any time off work.

W Oh, because of your business.

M Yes, I just don't get any vacations.

Q: Which is correct according to the conversation?

(a) The woman will visit Europe.

(b) The man often goes to New York.

(c) The woman cannot take a holiday.

(d) The man is running his own business.

43

M What kind of DVD shall we rent?

W Well, I'm not interested in horror films.

M What kind of film do you feel like?

W Something lighthearted and funny.

M So, I can't see an action movie.

W I'd prefer something else.

Q: What kind of film is the couple likely to watch?

(a) A zombie movie.

(b) A romantic comedy.

(c) A movie with action.

(d) A dramatic spy thriller.

44

M Hello, Sarah. How are things?

W Hi, Mike. Good. What's happening?

M I called to see if you wanted to go out for dinner.

W You mean tonight? I have to visit my parents.

M Oh, then how about tomorrow night?

W OK, I'm free then.

Q: What can be inferred about the woman from the conversation?

(a) She often calls the man.

(b) She can meet the man tonight.

(c) She will dine with the man tomorrow.

(d) She visits her parents most nights.

45

W Where can I get a good desk lamp?
M Maybe at the supermarket.
W There's not much choice there.
M Try the Internet, then.
W Do you know any good sites?
M No, but I'm sure there are plenty.

Q: What can be inferred from the conversation?
(a) The woman will shop online.
(b) The woman wants a pink lamp.
(c) The man works at a supermarket.
(d) The man will shop with the woman.

46

Another frosty night is expected tonight. Strong winds should add to the chill through early evening in Pennsylvania and further northward. Winds could exceed 10 miles per hour with a few gusts approaching 25 miles per hour. Overnight lows will drop into the 20s and 30s for much of the region. If you have to head out early, you may have to defrost the windshield. Some mountain valleys and plateau areas may be in for a hard freeze.

Q: What is the main idea of the weather report?
(a) It could be chilly tomorrow.
(b) It is going to be a cold night.
(c) It might be windy in Pennsylvania.
(d) It will be freezing for days to come.

47

I'm here to talk about wind energy. The use of wind turbines is growing because of many factors. Their operating costs are low and they are getting cheaper to build. Wind turbines produce no air or water pollution. They are very cost effective. As for harming wildlife, more birds are killed by cars, power lines, and high-rise buildings than by wind turbine blades. Because of its many advantages, governments are now encouraging the use of wind energy.

Q: What is the main idea about wind turbines?
(a) They produce cheap energy.
(b) They have a lot of benefits.
(c) They create energy from wind.
(d) They are promoted by government.

48

In my opinion, students need to be taught about the dangers of technology. The Internet provides a wealth of information, but students are at risk of getting incorrect information and using it wrongly. There is also a danger of students treating computers and the Internet as a form of entertainment rather than as tools for learning. They need to be taught how to use their time wisely and not be distracted.

Q: What is the talk mainly about?
(a) Why the Internet is dangerous.
(b) How students should use computers.
(c) Why students need to learn about technology.
(d) How technology can be misused by students.

49

As archaeology students, you might later have a career where you are studying human bones. In studying bones, you can learn a lot about our ancient ancestors. We can use techniques like radiocarbon dating and the analysis of ancient DNA, or we can look at atoms in bones and teeth to uncover other secrets. Using these techniques together, we can tell when and how a person died, their diet and family relationships, and even their travel experiences and place of birth.

Q: What is the main topic of the lecture?
(a) Methods of uncovering bones.
(b) Secrets of ancient ancestors.
(c) Types of careers in archaeology.
(d) Techniques for studying old bones.

50

In this class you have learned that birds are linked to dinosaurs. This has been further proven by scientists who studied fossils of the first known bird, which featured feather shapes. The impressions of the feathers are 150 million years old. And scientists found tiny amounts of chemicals in the feather impressions that are the same as the chemicals that exist in modern birds' feathers. This discovery is important because while scientists knew there was a physical link between birds and dinosaurs, now they also have a chemical link.

Q: What is the main idea about birds in the lecture?
(a) They existed with the dinosaurs.
(b) They had feathers 150 million years ago.
(c) They are chemically linked with dinosaurs.
(d) They have special chemicals in their feathers.

51

Hello everyone, I want to remind you about the new Middle School Math Circle program. The Middle School Math Circle is to help you develop math problem solving skills. You will be taught challenging mathematics beyond the normal curriculum. Math Circles are held on the first Saturdays of each month and the cost is $25 per student for each meeting. Middle School teachers are also welcome to attend at no cost with their students. I will put up more information on the school notice board.

Q: What is the announcement mainly about?
(a) Problem solving skills in math.
(b) A program for improving math skills.
(c) Math problems that students will do.
(d) A new institute for mathematics students.

52

Britain is experiencing the greatest emigration levels in recent history and a lot more Britons are thinking of moving abroad, a survey reveals. In the survey, three in ten Britons said the poor state of the economy was their reason for wanting to emigrate. Nearly a quarter of those surveyed blamed the lack of job prospects while an eighth said they simply wanted a change of lifestyle. The most popular destinations for Britons thinking of emigrating were Australia, New Zealand, France, and Spain.

Q: What is the news report mainly about?
(a) British standards of living.
(b) Immigrants now living in Britain.
(c) Britain's worsening economic conditions.
(d) People wanting to emigrate from Britain.

53

CompuTech stocks rose on Tuesday to close at $128.40 per share. That's nearly $2 above the record $126.60 level that CompuTech stocks were selling for on March 12. One reason for this was CompuTech's announcement that it would invest in video games. Another reason is that it is expected to release a new e-book device in coming months. The device will compete with top brands and will enable readers to browse an extensive free library of more than a million e-books, magazines, and newspapers.

Q: Which is correct about CompuTech according to the report?
(a) Its stock is at $126.60 a share.
(b) It plans to invest in video gaming.
(c) Its reading device has been released.
(d) It will provide e-books at a small cost.

54

We have studied satellite images of the upper Amazon region from 1999 and found evidence of 200 geometric patterns across a distance greater than 250 kilometers. We saw circles, squares, and other geometric shapes once hidden by forest. The shapes might date back as far as AD 200 to 300. These patterns are probably where buildings stood, and they suggest that a previously unknown ancient society once lived in the Amazon. The area possibly had as many as 60,000 people.

Q: Which is correct about the ground patterns according to the speaker?
(a) There were about 1,000 found.
(b) They were spread over more than 250 kilometers.
(c) There were no square shapes among them.
(d) They were where 200,000 people once lived.

55

Graduation season is right around the corner. So, celebrate the graduate in your life with colorful graduation flowers and gifts from Flowers To Go. We have all kinds of things for graduates, such as beautiful bouquets, toy bears, delicious treats, and even good luck plants for graduates who will move out of home. We are proud to offer a solution for any kind of graduation. We deliver across town or across the country. Call 1-800-FLOWERS now!

Q: Which is correct according to the advertisement?
(a) Most graduations have finished.
(b) Flowers To Go only sells flowers.
(c) Gifts such as toy bears are available.
(d) Flowers To Go can deliver internationally.

56

Hi, I am going to show you how to make a hot cocoa mix. You need a jar, and a measuring cup. What you do is mix together two and a half cups of powdered milk, one and a half cups of powdered sugar, one cup of coffee creamer, and one cup of cocoa powder. Mix all of the ingredients in a large bowl. Then pour everything into the jar. To make a cocoa drink, use three tablespoons of your mix per cup of hot water.

Q: Which is correct about making cocoa according to the instructions?
(a) Use five cups of powdered milk.
(b) Add in one cup of coffee creamer.
(c) Mix in three cups of cocoa powder.
(d) Make a drink with a teaspoon of mix.

57

I want to talk to you today about the increasing number of people diagnosed with adult-onset allergies. This is when adults catch allergies they never had before. The latest findings are that 1 in 3 adults in this country now suffer from some form of allergy, and this number is increasing by 5 percent each year. It didn't happen so much in the past. But these days we are seeing allergies starting in people in their 20s, 30s, or 40s. We don't know why, though.

Q: Which is correct according to the talk?
(a) Adult allergies are on the rise.
(b) Half of all adults have allergies.
(c) Adult allergy rates are in decline.
(d) People over 40 rarely get allergies.

58

I've mentioned before that children who have speech-impairing strokes often learn to talk again. However, adult stroke victims can lose the ability to talk for good. By examining the brains of child stroke victims, we've found that their brains rewire themselves. Other brain areas are used to make up for what was lost by the stroke. One child we examined had almost completely recovered in five years with absolutely no problems with his speech.

Q: What can be inferred from the talk?
(a) Children never have bad strokes.
(b) Adult brains cannot rewire easily.
(c) Some strokes actually improve language.
(d) Only one area in the brain is for speech.

59

This painting is called *Friends* and was painted by a new artist called Bernard Hampton. It is a complex painting featuring a man and woman seated together under a tree. What is interesting is that the man and woman do not seem to be friends, as the title of the painting suggests. If you look at them, it seems they are angry at each other. Their faces look tense, and they are looking away from each other with indifference. It is as if they have just had an argument.

Q: What can be inferred about the painting?
(a) Its title is ironic.
(b) It is worth a lot of money.
(c) Its colors are not very bright.
(d) It is the first Hampton ever painted.

60

For generations, Alaskan Natives have understood that survival of a group depends on the proper schooling of their youth. Their educational system is like an apprenticeship. Boys are taught by their uncles the skills to survive. Uncles carefully watch the boys. If a boy is good at a task, he is given more knowledge and responsibilities. That means boys have different levels of skill, even though they might be the same age. Their advancement is based on growth of character, physical development, and other abilities.

Q: What can be inferred about Alaskan Native schooling?
(a) Girls are schooled by aunts.
(b) Schooling ends at 15 years old.
(c) There are no class year levels.
(d) The largest boys always do best.

Actual Test 2

1

W How's the new assistant getting along?

M _____

(a) I think he did once.

(b) You two seem very close.

(c) She might go along with it.

(d) He seems to be doing well.

2

M Have you been to any concerts lately?

W _____

(a) No, too many to count.

(b) Not for quite some time.

(c) Sorry, I have plans tonight.

(d) My favorite band is Prodigy.

3

W I wish I could ride a motorcycle.

M _____

(a) That's OK. I don't mind.

(b) I can show you my bike.

(c) I will. It's interesting.

(d) Just try and learn.

4

M When will you finish your homework?

W _____

(a) Soon, I hope.

(b) Just a minute.

(c) Three hours ago.

(d) I've called it a day.

5

W I think Ryan looks just like his father.

M _____

(a) He certainly does.

(b) No, he's not a father yet.

(c) Yes, he has a twin brother.

(d) They don't see each other often.

6

M What brings you here?

W _____

(a) Let's take a cab.

(b) I didn't bring anything.

(c) I have an interview at 2.

(d) I'll take the subway instead.

7

W Excuse me. You dropped your key.

M _____

(a) I have a spare key.

(b) That's not what I wanted.

(c) Sorry, but that's not yours.

(d) Thanks. You're a lifesaver.

8

M Are you ready to order, ma'am?

W _____

(a) No, I've already paid.

(b) Today's special is salmon.

(c) Yes. Everything is in order.

(d) Just a chicken sandwich, please.

9

W Hello, can I speak to Alex?

M _____

(a) Thanks for taking my call.
(b) I'm returning Alex's call.
(c) I'm calling long distance.
(d) OK, hold the line, please.

10

M What are you doing tonight?

W _____

(a) I'll be free this afternoon.
(b) I'm just staying home.
(c) I'll see you tomorrow.
(d) I don't have anything.

11

W Sorry, there are no tables available right now.

M _____

(a) We will arrive earlier, then.
(b) That one would be perfect.
(c) In that case, we'll wait.
(d) These are all reserved.

12

M Do you have change for a $10 bill?

W _____

(a) Yes, I changed it already.
(b) I can, if that's OK with you.
(c) All right, you can leave a tip.
(d) No, but you could ask the cashier.

13

W I can't believe I got promoted to supervisor.

M _____

(a) Good for you.
(b) Maybe next time.
(c) I've been a supervisor.
(d) Anything you say is fine.

14

M This dish is to die for!

W _____

(a) You can have one.
(b) I feel bad about that.
(c) But no one passed away.
(d) I'll show you how to make it.

15

W Let's go out and get some fresh air.

M _____

(a) What a great idea!
(b) I'd rather go for a walk.
(c) I didn't mean to do that.
(d) How sweet of you to do that.

16

M Where's the hair dryer?
W Cathy took it with her.
M Then I'll just use a towel.
W _____

(a) I'll ask Cathy.
(b) Thanks, I will.
(c) Sorry about that.
(d) They're at the store.

17

W I can't access this site.
M You need to enter your password first.
W Could I use yours to sign in?
M _____

(a) You have to sign here.
(b) But I don't have a pen.
(c) A complicated password is safer.
(d) OK, but don't tell anyone what it is.

18

M Did you walk the dog?

W I was just about to do that.

M But where is he?

W _____

(a) I've already found him.

(b) Just here, under the table.

(c) I'll go and look over it all.

(d) Out taking a walk in the park.

19

W Didn't you bring your car to work?

M No. It's being repaired.

W Would you like a ride home?

M _____

(a) Yes, no need to worry.

(b) Well, it'll be done tomorrow.

(c) Sure, I can give you a lift home.

(d) Actually, my wife is picking me up.

20

M Why are you home so soon?

W School ended early today.

M Why is that?

W _____

(a) Around 2 o'clock.

(b) The bus arrived late.

(c) I was first to get there.

(d) A pipe burst in the building.

21

W Can you help me with this?

M Sure. What do you need?

W Just hold this stick here.

M _____

(a) OK. Tell me when.

(b) As soon as possible.

(c) I've been doing well.

(d) No problem. I can do that.

22

M Did you talk to Maria?

W Yes. I invited her to dinner.

M When did you arrange that for?

W _____

(a) Last week was the time.

(b) I scheduled it for Friday.

(c) Probably not in the future.

(d) She comes once in a while.

23

W What are you doing for the long weekend?

M I don't have any plans.

W You should come up to my cottage.

M _____

(a) I'm on my way to your place.

(b) Oh, I'm going away, then.

(c) That sounds like fun.

(d) I have to go now.

24

M Are you flying to Paris?

W I'm not sure yet.

M When will you know?

W _____

(a) I found out already.

(b) About 3 hours long.

(c) Sometime next week.

(d) It's early in the morning.

25

W Young man, what's your name?

M My name is Adam Weston.

W Aren't you supposed to be in class now?

M _____

(a) It's in the classroom.

(b) Down the hall, ma'am.

(c) My class already started.

(d) I have to see the principal.

26

M I can babysit for you.
W How much do you charge?
M I usually ask for $9 an hour.
W _____

(a) I'll take $10 for that.
(b) That sounds fair enough.
(c) You're asking for trouble.
(d) I have never been around children.

27

W I have to work late on Wednesday.
M Isn't Laura's piano recital on Wednesday?
W She said it's next Monday.
M _____

(a) That's what I meant, at 7 pm.
(b) Oh, I must have been mistaken.
(c) Well, she's not that good anyway.
(d) It will be held at the Civic Center.

28

M How was your date with Bob?
W Strange. He's very picky about what he eats.
M What did he have for dinner?
W _____

(a) Just a bowl of soup.
(b) We went to see a movie first.
(c) He doesn't know me very well.
(d) Unfortunately, I had a terrible time.

29

W I heard from Susie Jenkins today.
M Really? How's she doing?
W Her father passed away.
M _____

(a) Let's invite him over.
(b) I assumed it would be fine.
(c) She has been away too long.
(d) I'm really sorry to hear that.

30

M Did you find something you like?
W I like this red jacket.
M It's pretty expensive, though.
W _____

(a) I really thought so.
(b) No, it's quite pricey.
(c) Yes, it's a good deal.
(d) Actually, it's on sale.

31

W Hello, Carol's Catering. How may I help you?
M My office needs some food and drinks for a party.
W OK. How many people are you expecting?
M We're going to have around 200 employees.
W And where is this party being held?
M In one of our large conference rooms.

Q: What is the man mainly doing?
(a) Inquiring about catering prices.
(b) Inviting the woman to a party.
(c) Selling pre-cooked food items.
(d) Arranging catering for an event.

32

M Do you want to catch up this week?
W Monday night and Thursday night are good for me.
M I'm out of town on Monday, but Thursday is fine.
W Great. How's 7 o'clock for you?
M Perfect. Where should we go?
W Let's try the new Indian restaurant.

Q: What are the speakers mainly doing?
(a) Deciding on a restaurant.
(b) Arguing about what to do.
(c) Scheduling a time for a meal.
(d) Making plans to meet for dinner.

33

M I lost my call again!

W Switch to Zoop. It's the phone service I use.

M How much do you pay for your service?

W You'll like it. Its 600 minutes is $60 a month.

M Do you ever lose any calls?

W I've never lost a call with Zoop.

Q: What is the woman doing in the conversation?

(a) Telling the man to buy a new phone.

(b) Insisting that the man reduce his calls.

(c) Saying that the man cannot rely on Zoop.

(d) Advising the man to change phone services.

34

W Excuse me. Is there a library around here?

M No, but there's a bookstore nearby.

W Do you think they would have any old history books?

M Hmm. Perhaps you should try the City Historical Foundation.

W That's a good idea. Where's that?

M It's just a few blocks from here.

Q: What is the conversation mainly about?

(a) Locating the nearest bookstore.

(b) Directing someone to book sellers.

(c) Finding somewhere with history books.

(d) Walking to the City Historical Foundation.

35

M I booked my trip to Barcelona. I'm going next month.

W That's fantastic! You're going to love it there.

M What should I do while I'm there?

W Visit the Picasso Museum and see the architecture by Gaudi.

M Is there anything special I should eat in Barcelona?

W Yes, the tapas. Tapas are small plates of food.

Q: What is the woman mainly talking about?

(a) Museums to visit in Barcelona.

(b) Things to do in Barcelona.

(c) Art and architecture of Barcelona.

(d) Barcelona's most famous food.

36

M Hi, Francis. What's going on in the sales department?

W It's been hectic. How are things in accounting?

M Crazy. I have to get all the end-of-year sales figures done.

W It sounds like you're really busy these days.

M Yeah. I don't even have time to buy any Christmas gifts.

W I started my Christmas shopping early.

Q: What are the speakers talking about?

(a) Finishing accounting reports.

(b) Being really busy at work.

(c) Doing the Christmas shopping.

(d) Working in a new department.

37

M Hey, Mandy. How's your new business?

W Great. I got two more clients for a total of eight now.

M That's wonderful! How do you like being self-employed?

W It's great working from home. I can set my own hours.

M That sounds a lot better than my job.

W But at least you make a steady salary.

Q: What are the speakers mainly talking about?

(a) The man's job.

(b) The man's salary.

(c) The woman's clients.

(d) The woman's business.

38

W Congratulations on your promotion, Alex! Are you excited?

M Yes, but I hope I can handle all the responsibility.

W Of course you can. That's why you got the position.

M I guess so. Thanks for the vote of confidence.

W When do you start as vice president?

M Next week, though I wish I could have a break before I start.

Q: Which is correct about Alex according to the conversation?
(a) He got a job with no responsibility.
(b) He is thrilled about his promotion.
(c) He will work for the vice president.
(d) He is going on vacation next week.

39

M How can I help you today?
W I'd like to exchange this cell phone.
M I see. Is there something wrong with it?
W The numbers get stuck when I dial.
M OK, would you like the same model or a different one?
W I would like a different model, please.

Q: Which is correct according to the conversation?
(a) The man wants a cell phone refund.
(b) The woman's phone keypad sticks.
(c) The man cannot exchange the phone.
(d) The woman wants a same-phone exchange.

40

M I might take the subway instead of driving to work.
W The subway is so much faster than driving.
M Yes, and the subway's cheaper than paying for gas.
W Which subway station is closest to you?
M Osborne Station. It's 2 blocks away from me.
W You're lucky. The nearest subway station to me is 12 blocks away.

Q: Which is correct about the man according to the conversation?
(a) He has never driven to work before.
(b) He will spend less taking the subway.
(c) He resides 12 blocks from the subway.
(d) He lives a long way from a subway station.

41

W Can you believe it? The price of eggs has gone up again.
M I know. Even milk is more expensive these days.
W It's not just food. My electricity and gas bills are also higher.
M Everything is going up but our salaries.
W True. My family has already had to cut back on a lot of things.
M Us, too. We're going to have to cancel our cable television soon.

Q: Which is correct according to the conversation?
(a) The price of eggs is now lower.
(b) The cost of electricity has risen.
(c) The woman's salary has increased.
(d) The man stopped paying for cable TV.

42

W Sorry, could I use the outlet by your chair?
M I tried it earlier. Unfortunately, it doesn't work.
W It's impossible for me to work if I can't plug in my laptop.
M There's an outlet by the coffee shop restrooms.
W Oh, yeah? Maybe I'll move over there.
M You need to order something to drink first, though.

Q: What can be inferred from the conversation?
(a) The woman will go to the restroom.
(b) The man will leave the coffee shop.
(c) The woman will order something to drink.
(d) The man will not be able to use his laptop.

43

W All our diamonds are handpicked by the manager.

M Everything is beautiful, but I'm not sure what to get my wife.

W She can come back to exchange an item if she doesn't like it.

M That sounds reasonable. How much is this ring here?

W That one is $2,000. The diamond is just over one carat.

M I hope it will convince her to forgive me.

Q: What can be inferred about the man?
(a) He is choosing a necklace.
(b) He wants to apologize to his wife.
(c) He would like to exchange an item.
(d) He is looking for an engagement ring.

44

M Amy, how's work on your new building going?

W Not that great. We still have three more apartments to paint.

M Have you rented all the apartments yet?

W Only five of them. I put ads for the other three on the Internet.

M When are your tenants going to move in?

W April 1. I still have to put in the carpets, too.

Q: What can be inferred from the conversation?
(a) The woman is a landlord.
(b) The woman has eight tenants.
(c) The man lives in Amy's building.
(d) The man will move in next month.

45

W Neil! Long time no see. How are you?

M Great, Jessica. How're Roger and the kids?

W Everyone is doing well. Roger loves his new job.

M I'm so happy to hear that.

W We should get together for dinner soon and catch up.

M I'll talk to Liz. She'd love to have you and Roger over for dinner.

Q: What can be inferred from the conversation?
(a) Liz has not met Neil before.
(b) Neil and Roger work together.
(c) Jessica is looking for a new job.
(d) Roger and Jessica have children.

46

Is your dog always running away? Are you afraid it might get hit by a car? Then contact InvisiBorder. InvisiBorder is an invisible barrier around your yard. It'll keep your dog on your property just like a real fence would. Your dog can run around the yard and you don't have to worry about it running away. Best of all, InvisiBorder is cheaper than erecting a real fence around your yard. For more information, visit www.InvisiBorder.com.

Q: What is being advertised?
(a) A product for a pet.
(b) A new type of dog food.
(c) A cheap dog-walking service.
(d) An innovative home repair service.

47

Our city is putting up new buildings. This means they're cutting down a lot of trees. But animals depend on plants and trees for food and shelter. We can already see that the population of monarch butterflies is decreasing because of the loss of plants and trees. They usually nest on the branches of trees. The female butterflies lay their eggs on a plant called milkweed. However, as the city continues to develop, the butterflies lose more of their habitat. Soon the whole monarch butterfly species could be lost.

Q: What is the speaker mainly talking about?
(a) An alternative to cutting down trees.
(b) Urban development plans for a city.
(c) The impact of development on a species.
(d) The mating rituals of monarch butterflies.

48

Hello, this message is for Adam Gomez. My name is Chris DeMilo with Premium Auto. You called about a quote for your Hyundai Sonata. I've reviewed your information, and we could insure this vehicle for $720 a year. If you prefer, you could pay $70 a month. This price includes discounts for having a good driving record for the past 10 years. If you have any questions, I'd be happy to answer them. You can reach me at 342-3033.

Q: What is the message mainly about?
(a) Selling a used vehicle.
(b) Buying a new Hyundai car.
(c) Informing of insurance prices.
(d) Confirming an appointment.

49

If a bee stings you, tell one of your parents or an adult immediately. This is because some people are allergic to bee stings. Otherwise, you can simply treat the sting. Start by removing the bee's stinger at once, if the bee has left its stinger behind. Wash the area with soap and water. You can also put ice on the area. This will relieve the swelling and make it hurt less. Of course, try to prevent bee stings in the first place. Do not try and drive a bee away because this only makes them angry.

Q: What is the speaker mainly talking about?
(a) Removing a bee's stinger.
(b) Dealing with bee stings.
(c) Curing bee allergies.
(d) Preventing attacks by bees.

50

Please allow me to talk about my experience. First, I've worked for five years in this industry. I believe that my supervisors value me. My co-workers respect me as well. Second, I am a hard worker. I come to work on time and I always meet my deadlines. Third, I am talented at what I do. At my last job, I was named Employee of the Month three times. I am very confident about my skills. In short, I believe I am the right person for this job.

Q: What is the speaker mainly talking about?
(a) His previous job experience.
(b) Why he is qualified for the job.
(c) His awards won while in other positions.
(d) Why he was the Employee of the Month.

51

Good afternoon, passengers. Please be sure to exchange your ticket for a boarding pass before you board the train. Boarding passes are available now at the booth next to Gate 11. If you need to buy a ticket, please make your way to the ticket window. You can also use one of our automated ticket machines in the lobby. Keep in mind you can access the platform only after receiving a boarding pass. The train to Hartford will arrive in 15 minutes. Boarding will begin at 1:40. Thank you.

Q: What is the announcement mainly about?
(a) The latest arrival information.
(b) The automation of train ticketing.
(c) The way to obtain train schedules.
(d) The procedure for boarding a train.

52

I'm very pleased to introduce our next speaker, Dr. Sonia Patek from the University of New Delhi. Dr. Patek has published numerous reports on a variety of vitamins. Today, she will discuss her research on vitamin C and present her findings from recent experiments. She and her team investigated the effects of too much vitamin C on the body's immune system. Dr. Patek was recently elected to the Board of Directors of the Panel of Worldwide Nutritionists. Please give a warm welcome to Dr. Patek.

Q: What will be the main focus of Dr. Patek's talk?
(a) Best brands of vitamins to buy.
(b) Aspects of her scientific career.
(c) Results from her vitamin research.
(d) Problems with the immune system.

53

Hello, my name is Allison Spears. I'm the director of Good Hope. We accept donations of used clothing, blankets, and linens. We also accept items for the kitchen such as toasters, cooking utensils, and dishes. If you would like to donate something, please look for one of these stands in your neighborhood and place your things inside it. Someone from Good Hope will come once a week to collect all the items. Many families would really appreciate anything you can give. Please find it in your heart to give hope to somebody.

Q: What is the speaker asking people to do?

(a) Donate food to flood victims.
(b) Help the homeless with donations.
(c) Raise money for a worthwhile charity.
(d) Give unwanted goods to those in need.

54

Welcome to the 29th annual Pottery Conference. If you have pre-registered, you may pick up your conference badge and information packet at the rear of the room. If you still need to register, come down to the front of the room. Please be sure to wear your badge at all times. You will need it to enter all conference sessions. The first conference will start in 15 minutes in the Grand Ballroom. Anyone with questions can visit the information booth. Look for the red "Information" sign.

Q: Which is correct according to the announcement?

(a) The Pottery Conference is organized every two years.
(b) An information pack is available before registering.
(c) The first conference talk is currently underway.
(d) An information booth is set up for questions.

55

Our next contestant is a 42-year-old doctor from Kalamazoo. Her specialty is in healing broken bones. She was born in China and moved to this country when she was eight. After completing medical school at Lakeside University in Chicago, she got married. She now has an 8-year-old son and a 6-year-old daughter. She says that if she wins the grand prize, she will take her family to visit China. Ladies and gentleman, please welcome today's guest, Lily Yuen!

Q: Which is correct about the woman according to the talk?

(a) She lives in Chicago.
(b) She has two children.
(c) She won the grand prize.
(d) She has never been to China.

56

This is Manny Wilson with your WKVG news update. The President signed a bill that will raise the salary of school teachers by an average of 4.8 percent nationwide. He said this would help stimulate the country's education system. In local news, Mayor Cowell said she will not approve a proposed $1 billion plan for new streetcars. She believes that the bill will not help with traffic congestion. Stay tuned for WKVG weather and traffic right after this word from our sponsor.

Q: Which is correct according to the news report?

(a) The President raised the minimum wage.
(b) The President increased the pay for teachers.
(c) The mayor does not approve of the President's plan.
(d) The mayor approved a new bill for traffic congestion.

57

A kibbutz is a collective farm or settlement owned by its members in Israel. The members raise children together. It was created as a place for Jews to live and work together. It is a place without private property and everything is shared, even work, tools, and clothing. When originally formed, the kibbutzim, which is the plural for kibbutz, did not need funding. But eventually they had to rely on support from charities and now the Israeli government provides aid.

Q: Which is correct according to the talk?
(a) Children are not allowed at a kibbutz.
(b) Members of a kibbutz divide the labor.
(c) Kibbutz members must share their money.
(d) Kibbutzim no longer need financial assistance.

58

In Lewis Carroll's *Alice in Wonderland*, the main character, Alice, falls through a rabbit hole. After a while, she lands in a strange world with bizarre characters. A lot of the story is symbolic, but most children will find it difficult to figure out what he was trying to symbolize with the various characters and objects in the story. So while many children read this story, Carroll's symbolic references are more likely to be enjoyed by mature readers.

Q: What will be talked about next?
(a) A summary of Carroll's story.
(b) Other books written by Lewis Carroll.
(c) Examples of symbolism in *Alice in Wonderland*.
(d) Reasons why children love *Alice in Wonderland*.

59

At the end of the Second World War, Germany was divided into two countries, East and West Germany. The Soviets brutally controlled the East and West Germany became a wealthy democracy supported by the United States. The former capital city of Berlin was also divided in two. In 1961, the East Germans built a wall to separate East Berlin from West Berlin. Nobody could freely cross the Berlin Wall and no one was allowed to cross it. Those who attempted to cross were captured or killed. In November 1989, the Berlin Wall fell and free travel was allowed once again.

Q: What can be inferred from the talk?
(a) Many Berliners became US citizens after WWII.
(b) East Germans built the wall but the US paid for it.
(c) West Germans did not want the Berlin Wall to fall.
(d) Mostly East Germans were killed at the Berlin Wall.

60

This is Pat Connelly from the KQED traffic center. Most roadways are flowing smoothly at this hour. Highway 1 was a little slow from downtown to Petaluma because of an earlier stalled vehicle. That has now been cleared to the shoulder. Construction near Exit 20 on the Belt Parkway is causing some congestion. And we're just getting word of an overturned truck on Lincoln Bridge. All in all, though, things look better than usual for your evening commute. We'll be back with more details in 30 minutes.

Q: What can be inferred from the traffic report?
(a) Most people are on their way to work.
(b) Drivers should stay clear of Highway 1.
(c) Commuters should avoid Lincoln Bridge.
(d) Belt Parkway's construction is nearly finished.

Actual Test 3

1

M   Where's David?

W   _____

(a) He's at home.
(b) He's studying.
(c) Around nine o'clock.
(d) Probably after school.

2

W   There's only some leftover sandwich from yesterday.

M   _____

(a) You are always thinking about food.
(b) Thanks but I already ate my lunch.
(c) There's some sand on the beach.
(d) In that case, let's just eat out.

3

M   When is the party?

W   _____

(a) I hope so.
(b) It's for Dan.
(c) It's at my house.
(d) It's this Saturday.

4

W   Daniel is in the market for a new car.

M   _____

(a) He should contact Manny at my dealership.
(b) His new car must have been expensive.
(c) Gasoline prices are at an all-time high.
(d) The market isn't very far from here.

5

W   Are you taking the bus?

M   _____

(a) No, I'm going to walk there.
(b) Sure, every 15 minutes.
(c) Yes, you've been waiting a long time.
(d) No, it takes longer than that to get there.

6

W   What do you think of this dress?

M   _____

(a) It looks too big on you.
(b) It costs 100 dollars plus tax.
(c) I bought it at a department store.
(d) I need ten minutes to get dressed.

7

M   When you drive around here, be careful of the wild animals.

W   _____

(a) I don't know how to drive.
(b) I'll do it right away.
(c) Please take care of yourself.
(d) Thanks for the warning.

8

W   You're in awfully good spirits!

M   _____

(a) The weather is unpredictable these days.
(b) Yeah, you should feel awful about that.
(c) The church service starts at 11 a.m.
(d) Lisa just told me a funny story.

9

M　Where should I drop you off?

W　_____

(a) At the corner is fine.
(b) Sure. Thanks for the ride.
(c) I'll let you out at the next block.
(d) Sorry, but I can't drop it off today.

10

W　Could you come down a bit on the price?

M　_____

(a) I'll take ten dollars off.
(b) Yes, it's fairly inexpensive.
(c) You put a lot of work into it.
(d) The price is too high for me.

11

W　Do you want some help with that?

M　_____

(a) I do that every time.
(b) That was very helpful.
(c) I'm sorry but I can't right now.
(d) I would very much, thank you.

12

W　You haven't started your homework yet, have you?

M　_____

(a) Actually, I have.
(b) It starts in two hours.
(c) I have math homework.
(d) My parents are at work now.

13

M　How long will the train ride be?

W　_____

(a) The service is pretty good on the train.
(b) It's about three hours one way.
(c) It's a smooth ride all the way.
(d) I'll be away for two weeks.

14

W　Hello, is Alice there, please?

M　_____

(a) Yes, I can see why.
(b) Sure, I'll go get her.
(c) Yes, put her through.
(d) I'm sorry, she's right here.

15

W　How did you like the movie?

M　_____

(a) It was in a new theater.
(b) You seem to like it a lot.
(c) I enjoyed the action scenes.
(d) Kids don't like movies today.

16

M　What's that noise?
W　Mary is crying out loud.
M　Why is she crying?
W　_____

(a) She's here.
(b) She's happy.
(c) Her dog died.
(d) It's her birthday.

17

M　Where are you going now?
W　I'm going to the bank.
M　What are you going to do there?
W　_____

(a) The doctor's appointment is at 2 o'clock.
(b) There's a bank machine on the corner.
(c) They need some work done there.
(d) I need to deposit a check.

18

M   What are you doing?

W   I'm sewing.

M   I didn't know you could sew.

W   _____

(a) There are so many things.

(b) Actually, I don't need any.

(c) It's so difficult for you and me.

(d) Well, just simple things like a button.

19

M   What are you going to order?

W   I'm not sure yet. What do you suggest?

M   The chicken here is delicious.

W   _____

(a) Then that's what I'll get.

(b) I've never cooked it here.

(c) I don't like fish very much.

(d) It's great that you enjoyed it.

20

W   Should we bring over a cake for Janet?

M   I was just going to pick up some flowers.

W   Yeah, that's a better idea.

M   _____

(a) She has enough flour for the cake.

(b) Janet grows flowers in her garden.

(c) I know Janet likes pink roses.

(d) I'm allergic to flowers.

21

W   Make sure to read it over before signing.

M   I already reviewed everything at home.

W   Wonderful. Do you have any questions?

M   _____

(a) I used to ask a lot of questions as a student.

(b) More time to read it would be helpful.

(c) You have too many questions for me.

(d) No, everything is pretty clear.

22

M   The art gallery has an interesting exhibit.

W   I've been meaning to check it out.

M   I'd be willing to go again with you.

W   _____

(a) Many people are interested in it.

(b) That artist has a loyal fan base.

(c) I have time next weekend.

(d) I already saw it last week.

23

M   Hi, I'm looking to buy a new printer.

W   How much do you want to spend?

M   Not more than $150.

W   _____

(a) Printers are important in an office.

(b) We have a few in that range.

(c) That's the one that I have.

(d) OK, let me think about it.

24

M   Did you see the fireworks last night?

W   Fireworks? Where did you see them?

M   There was a fireworks show at the harbor.

W   _____

(a) Yes, they were dazzling to watch.

(b) I guess I missed the show.

(c) I hope nobody was hurt.

(d) I see them all the time.

25

W   Do you have plans this weekend?

M   No, is there something going on?

W   I thought we could go out dancing.

M   _____

(a) I'm out of town this weekend.

(b) That sounds like a terrific idea!

(c) I wanted to try that restaurant, too.

(d) I would love to take a dancing lesson.

26

W You look very happy today.
M I just got some great news.
W You did? Tell me about it!
M _____

(a) I got the job I applied for.
(b) My girlfriend broke up with me.
(c) I'm moving away in a few months.
(d) I tried a new place for lunch today.

27

M How do you like your classes this semester?
W They're a bit difficult but I'm learning a lot.
M Yeah, I'm having a hard time in economics.
W _____

(a) I don't know if I can afford it.
(b) We're currently in a recession.
(c) That professor is especially tough.
(d) I'm usually right about these things.

28

M You got this package in the mail.
W Yes, I've been waiting for this for weeks.
M So what have you got there?
W _____

(a) It's the T-shirt I ordered.
(b) I'm not really sure what it is.
(c) I have to send it by tomorrow.
(d) It takes three days to get there.

29

M Good, I got you before you left the house.
W I was just about to leave. What's up?
M Could you bring me the bag I lent you?
W _____

(a) Sorry, I ate it for breakfast.
(b) Thank you for lending it to me.
(c) Yes, I should've returned it sooner.
(d) Of course you can borrow my bag.

30

W Are there any computers available now?
M Yes, how long would you like to use it?
W I just need it for one hour.
M _____

(a) Unfortunately, they're all occupied at the moment.
(b) The technician will need 30 minutes to repair it.
(c) You can sit at terminal 15 over there.
(d) I'm looking for a reliable person.

31

W Hello, this is WinEx. How may I help you?
M Hi, I have a question about a shipment.
W I would be happy to help you with that.
M I was expecting a delivery today, but it's not here yet.
W Do you have the tracking number for your order?
M Ihave it right here. The number is AKE43424743.

Q: What is the man mainly doing?
(a) Placing an order for delivery.
(b) Asking where his shipment is.
(c) Sending a package to someone.
(d) Changing the address on a shipment.

32

M Let's go see a movie together. Are you free next week?
W That sounds fun. I could go either Tuesday or Friday.
M I have plans on Tuesday. Friday works for me, though.
W All right. I'll find out what's playing that night.
M Great. Which theater are you thinking of going to?
W I thought we could go to Cineville on Main Street.

Q: What are the man and woman mainly doing?
(a) Buying movie tickets.
(b) Disagreeing about plans.
(c) Deciding on a day to meet.
(d) Arguing about which movie is better.

33

W Hi, can you tell me where the nearest hardware store is?

M There isn't one close to here. What are you looking for?

W I need to get some duct tape for a project I'm working on.

M I believe they sell that at Shopper's Market.

W That's good to know. Where's the nearest one?

M It's two blocks from here in that direction.

Q: What is the conversation mainly about?
(a) Finding some duct tape.
(b) The nearest hardware store.
(c) Directions to the drugstore.
(d) One of the woman's projects.

34

M I've decided to go to Iceland for vacation.

W I had a fantastic time there last summer.

M Do you have any recommendations for things to do there?

W You must go horseback riding around the Blue Lagoon.

M Any special food I should try?

W Try the fermented shark.

Q: What is the woman mainly talking about?
(a) Specialty food in Iceland.
(b) Flights to and from Iceland.
(c) Riding horses around a lagoon.
(d) Things to do in a foreign country.

35

M You seem upset about something.

W Dan's been giving me way too much work lately.

M Things have been busy for me, too.

W I'm exhausted all the time.

M We're in a busy period now.

W I hope it'll be over soon before I burn out.

Q: What are the speakers talking about?
(a) Problems they have with their boss.
(b) Working conditions at their job.
(c) Getting together with friends.
(d) Finding new work to do.

36

M Olga, how's it going? Have you found a new apartment yet?

W Yes, I actually found a wonderful place close to work.

M That's great! When are you going to move?

W My lease starts June 1, but I'm going to move in the weekend before.

M Do you need help with your move? I could lend you a hand.

W Thanks so much for offering, but I'm going to hire movers.

Q: What are the speakers mainly talking about?
(a) Living close to the office.
(b) Plans to move into a new place.
(c) Searching for a new apartment.
(d) Hiring workers to help with a move.

37

W Did you hear about subway and bus fares?

M Yeah, I can't believe they're going up.

W I wouldn't mind if the services got better.

M I want to just save up and buy a car.

W But gasoline prices are going up as well.

M This city is getting too expensive.

Q: Which is correct according to the conversation?
(a) The man is thinking about selling his car.
(b) The man is going to move to another city.
(c) The woman and man work in the same office.
(d) The woman is unhappy with public transit in her city.

38

W Have they announced who the new director of marketing will be?

M Not yet, but I hope they give the position to Sherry.

W She'd be great. However, I heard they want to hire someone from outside.

M They should encourage people to work hard and rise up the ranks.

W I agree. Otherwise this company will lose valuable employees.

M I think Sherry will leave if she doesn't get this promotion.

Q: Which is correct about Sherry according to the conversation?
(a) She recently received a promotion.
(b) She works with the man and woman.
(c) She is planning to leave the company.
(d) She has been with the company for a short time.

39

M Hi, can I help you with something today?
W I'm having some problems with this camera.
M I'm sorry to hear that. What seems to be wrong with it?
W When I turn off the camera the zoom lens won't go back in.
M Our technician can look at it but it will cost you $50.
W I need to use it today, so whatever it takes to make it work.

Q: Which is correct according to the conversation?
(a) The man will fix the camera.
(b) Service repairs are free of charge.
(c) The camera does not work properly.
(d) The woman is returning the camera for a refund.

40

M Hey, is that a new bicycle?
W I actually bought this used from an ad on Mikeslist.
M I've heard of Mikeslist but never bought anything from it.
W You can find great deals on it.
M I've been looking for a cheap bike myself.
W I saw plenty of ads for used bikes.

Q: Which is correct according to the conversation?
(a) The man wants to buy a bicycle.
(b) The woman is a bicycle vendor.
(c) The man sold his bike to the woman.
(d) The woman likes to sell items on Mikeslist.

41

M Do you need a ride to Jim's recital tonight or are you OK?
W Oh, no! I totally forgot that was tonight.
M Are you still coming or did you make other plans?
W I made dinner plans, but I promised Jim I would be there.
M Just finish your dinner before the recital ends.
W It's going to be tight, but I guess I could do that.

Q: How does the man suggest the woman solve the problem?
(a) Apologize to Jim in advance of the recital.
(b) Cancel the dinner plans the woman made.
(c) Attend the recital after her dinner.
(d) Go to the recital before dinner.

42

W Hi, Mark. Have you started your history paper?
M Funny you should ask. I just started it today.
W Lucky you. What're you doing your paper on?
M It's on the role of women during World War II.
W I wish I could think of a topic that interesting.
M Let's think of something together.

Q: What can be inferred from the conversation?
(a) The woman has not started her paper yet.
(b) The man will get a good grade on his paper.
(c) The man and woman are doing a paper together.
(d) The woman has already finished writing her paper.

43

W   Look at those clouds.We should probably move the party indoors.

M   What if we put up some tents? That will keep people dry.

W   Yes, but the ground will be muddy and ruin people's shoes.

M   I suppose you're right. Should we start moving stuff now?

W   We might as well while it's still dry out.

M   All right, I'll ask the workers to help move the tables.

Q: What can be inferred from the conversation?

(a) It is raining right now.

(b) The weather is clearing up.

(c) The wedding will move indoors.

(d) The speakers are preparing for an event.

44

M   It's getting late. I'm going to get ready for bed now.

W   I'm exhausted, but I'm going to wait up for Belinda.

M   Are you sure? It sounded like she'd be home really late.

W   Iwon't be able to sleep until I hear her big news, though.

M   I'm too tired. I'll have to hear the details in the morning.

W   Suit yourself, but it's not every day that someone gets engaged.

Q: What can be inferred from the conversation?

(a) Belinda is going to get married.

(b) The woman is Belinda's mother.

(c) Belinda will not be home till the morning.

(d) The man is going to propose to someone soon.

45

W   Have you called a plumber yet?

M   No, I don't think that's necessary.

W   We need a professional to fix the toilet.

M   I can take care of it.

W   Fix it and I won't argue with you.

M   Fine. I'll take a look at it now.

Q: What can be inferred from the conversation?

(a) The man has trained as a plumber.

(b) The woman will pay for the plumber.

(c) The man believes he can fix the problem.

(d) The woman will call a professional to their home.

46

Have peace of mind with Pet Partners' services. We offer daily walks for your dog and care for your pets when you're away. We keep all your pet's information on file. We also keep track of what your pet likes to eat and do. Our service includes pick-up and drop-off. All our staff members are trained to provide the best care for your pet. Call us now to arrange for a home visit.

Q: What is being advertised?

(a) A pet sitter.

(b) A new pet food.

(c) An animal doctor.

(d) A pet grooming service.

47

In homes across this country, people turn on their faucets and water comes out. We need to do our part to protect this natural resource. We cannot continue to pollute streams and rivers if we want to have a steady supply of water. Make sure to throw away toxic substances properly. Do not flush them down the toilet. Conserve water when you can because water is precious. We should try not to waste it.

Q: What is the talk mainly about?

(a) The problem of pollution in cities.

(b) Sinks and faucets in people's homes.

(c) Saving a natural resource we rely on.

(d) The best places to throw away garbage.

48

Hi, this message is for Cory Shuster. I saw your ad online for the two-bedroom apartment on Windsor Road. The apartment sounds exactly like what my roommate and I are looking to rent. We'd love to schedule a time to come look at your place. We work during the day but can visit anytime after 6 p.m. on weekdays and anytime on weekends. You can reach me on my cell phone at 647-378-4943.

Q: What is the message mainly about?
(a) Selling an apartment.
(b) Looking for a roommate.
(c) Arranging to view a place.
(d) The caller's work schedule.

49

At some point in your life you have probably gotten a splinter. Splinters are usually harmless, but it's still important to remove them as soon as possible. Left untreated, they might sink further into your skin. First, wash the area with soap and water. Then dry it thoroughly. You can usually remove a splinter with a pair of tweezers. If it looks infected, go and see a doctor immediately.

Q: What is the speaker mainly talking about?
(a) The best tweezers to use for splinters.
(b) A method for getting rid of a splinter.
(c) Seeing a doctor about a splinter.
(d) Being careful with wood.

50

Some forms of baldness are genetic and cannot be prevented. Other types can be treated. Eating a healthy diet rich in fruit, vegetables, and nuts can help hair to grow. You can also decrease hair loss by taking care of your hair properly. Strong shampoos and hair products can damage the hair. Stick to gentle products such as baby shampoo. Wet hair can also break easily so do not brush or comb your hair when it's wet.

Q: What is the passage about?
(a) How to best treat baldness.
(b) Advice on preventing hair loss.
(c) The causes that lead to losing hair.
(d) Hair products for fighting baldness.

51

Attention, passengers. We're being held momentarily in the station due to a stalled train ahead of us. The snowstorm has dumped snow on the tracks and that train is currently stuck in a snowbank. Track technicians have been called to the site. However, many roads are blocked and it may take them some time to arrive. We apologize for the delay and any inconvenience this may cause you. We will keep you updated on any developments.

Q: What is the announcement mainly about?
(a) A delay in service.
(b) The train schedule.
(c) An alternate train route.
(d) The bad weather conditions.

52

I'm thrilled to introduce our next speaker. Bob Canter has been called the Godfather of Real Estate. He was responsible for developing properties such as Canter Towers and Canter Palace. He's just published a book called *The Art of Real Estate*. Today, he's going to tell us what it takes to make it in today's real estate market. I'm sure you will learn a lot about closing your own real estate deals. Please welcome Bob Canter!

Q: What will Bob Canter talk about?
(a) Managing his properties.
(b) Publishing his new book.
(c) Being successful in real estate.
(d) How to become a millionaire quickly.

53

Many people in this city do not have homes or food. You can find out about the homeless situation and how you can help. By simply buying a copy of *Street News* magazine, you are supporting the city's homeless shelters. The money will go directly to feeding and housing the homeless. Each issue costs just two dollars and will help those who need it most. Thank you for your time.

Q: What is the speaker asking people to do?
(a) Purchase a magazine.
(b) Prepare food for the homeless.
(c) Volunteer at a homeless shelter.
(d) Donate money to an organization.

54

Some plants have flowers while others do not. Plants that have flowers have seeds in their fruit. One type of fruit is berries and these include tomatoes and grapes. Berries have seeds that are embedded in the flesh of the fruit. A second type of fruit is called drupes. They have one seed enclosed in a hard case surrounded by flesh. Peaches and plums are examples of drupes.

Q: What is the difference between the two types of fruits?
(a) The firmness of the flesh varies.
(b) The types of seeds they have.
(c) The kinds of flowers they produce.
(d) One is sweet while the other is sour.

55

Paris is the most visited city in the world. With all its famous landmarks and museums, which contain centuries of history, it's no wonder. You have probably read about these places or seen them in movies. Then there is the excellent food that can be enjoyed throughout the city. Paris is best seen on foot, whether you walk along the Seine River or through countless charming alleyways.

Q: Which is correct according to the travel review?
(a) Paris is known for its historic buildings.
(b) The rivers are especially lovely in Paris.
(c) There is a shortage of restaurants in Paris.
(d) Many cities have more attractions than Paris.

56

Things are still moving slowly on Highway 1. Drivers are advised to take Interstate 10 instead. All roads to the airport are also backed up. Give yourself an extra 20 minutes if you're headed in that direction. Otherwise, most roads are moving smoothly for the evening rush hour. This is Chris Parcell with KTDE Live Traffic. Now back to Pauline in the studio.

Q: Which is correct according to the news report?
(a) There was an accident on Interstate 10.
(b) There is construction on Highway 1.
(c) Most roads are clear this morning.
(d) Traffic is slow going to the airport.

57

The Chocolate War is an example of realistic fiction. This is a genre that has stories about situations in the real world. This does not mean that the events in the story actually did happen. It simply means that they could happen. Therefore, realistic fiction cannot consist of any magic or fantasy. At the most, it can have unusual events or exaggerated characters.

Q: Which is correct according to the lecture?
(a) The genre mentioned does not have elements of fantasy.
(b) Realistic fiction is the preferred genre among authors.
(c) Unusual events often take place in realistic fiction.
(d) Events in realistic fiction are those that took place.

58

You may have heard of the director Alfred Hitchcock. Perhaps you know some of his films, such as *Psycho, Rear Window*, or *Vertigo*. Hitchcock had a long career. He made 53 feature-length films and worked with many different actors. People called him the master of suspense because of the way he was able to surprise and scare viewers. Another special trait of his movies is his use of blonde actresses. He worked with some of the most popular actresses of the time.

Q: What will be talked about next?

(a) The men in Hitchcock's movies.
(b) Hitchcock's most popular movies.
(c) Awards given to Alfred Hitchcock.
(d) Some of the actresses in Hitchcock's films.

59

Hundreds of people have been scammed by a buyer on a popular online bidding site called eBay. The man ran a scam in which he sent checks to sellers for more than the price asked for. He would then ask sellers to return the excess amount. Banks cashed the checks right away but later found out that the checks were invalid. The man made over $100,000 this way. Police are still trying to find this man.

Q: What can be inferred about the man from the talk?

(a) He is currently in a lot of debt.
(b) He has been arrested by the police.
(c) He was addicted to online shopping.
(d) He issued fake checks to make money.

60

The next time your doctor recommends a surgical procedure, get a second opinion from another doctor. A study shows that not all surgery is necessary. For example, many pregnant women had surgery to deliver babies. Tests afterward showed that they could have given birth naturally. The doctors chose to operate because it took less time and earned them more money. Other research found that 90% of all cases of back surgery are ineffective.

Q: Which of the following can be inferred from the talk?

(a) Patients are choosing to have surgery more often.
(b) Doctors should be more careful before operating.
(c) More women would like to have babies naturally.
(d) Surgery is an effective treatment for many conditions.

Actual Test 1

Answer Keys

🎧 Listening Comprehension

1	(c)	7	(d)	13	(c)	19	(d)	25	(c)	31	(b)	37	(d)	43	(b)	49	(d)	55	(c)
2	(d)	8	(c)	14	(b)	20	(b)	26	(b)	32	(d)	38	(c)	44	(c)	50	(c)	56	(b)
3	(d)	9	(d)	15	(c)	21	(d)	27	(a)	33	(d)	39	(b)	45	(a)	51	(b)	57	(a)
4	(c)	10	(b)	16	(b)	22	(c)	28	(c)	34	(c)	40	(c)	46	(b)	52	(d)	58	(b)
5	(a)	11	(d)	17	(a)	23	(b)	29	(b)	35	(c)	41	(c)	47	(b)	53	(b)	59	(a)
6	(b)	12	(b)	18	(d)	24	(d)	30	(b)	36	(b)	42	(d)	48	(d)	54	(b)	60	(c)

📝 Grammar

1	(b)	6	(a)	11	(c)	16	(b)	21	(c)	26	(b)	31	(d)	36	(a)	41	(b)	46	(d)
2	(b)	7	(a)	12	(a)	17	(c)	22	(c)	27	(c)	32	(a)	37	(b)	42	(b)	47	(d)
3	(d)	8	(d)	13	(d)	18	(c)	23	(c)	28	(d)	33	(c)	38	(a)	43	(c)	48	(b)
4	(d)	9	(b)	14	(d)	19	(a)	24	(c)	29	(c)	34	(c)	39	(c)	44	(c)	49	(c)
5	(d)	10	(c)	15	(c)	20	(b)	25	(b)	30	(d)	35	(d)	40	(d)	45	(d)	50	(b)

📢 Vocabulary

1	(d)	6	(a)	11	(c)	16	(b)	21	(d)	26	(c)	31	(c)	36	(d)	41	(d)	46	(d)
2	(c)	7	(c)	12	(d)	17	(a)	22	(b)	27	(b)	32	(d)	37	(b)	42	(a)	47	(b)
3	(b)	8	(d)	13	(c)	18	(b)	23	(b)	28	(c)	33	(b)	38	(b)	43	(b)	48	(c)
4	(c)	9	(a)	14	(a)	19	(a)	24	(b)	29	(c)	34	(d)	39	(d)	44	(c)	49	(b)
5	(b)	10	(d)	15	(c)	20	(a)	25	(d)	30	(d)	35	(b)	40	(d)	45	(c)	50	(d)

✒ Reading Comprehension

1	(a)	5	(b)	9	(b)	13	(c)	17	(b)	21	(d)	25	(b)	29	(c)	33	(c)	37	(b)
2	(c)	6	(a)	10	(a)	14	(b)	18	(d)	22	(c)	26	(c)	30	(b)	34	(b)	38	(c)
3	(b)	7	(b)	11	(b)	15	(b)	19	(b)	23	(d)	27	(b)	31	(b)	35	(c)	39	(a)
4	(c)	8	(d)	12	(d)	16	(c)	20	(b)	24	(a)	28	(b)	32	(b)	36	(b)	40	(d)

Actual Test 2

Answer Keys

🎧 Listening Comprehension

1	(d)	7	(d)	13	(a)	19	(d)	25	(d)	31	(d)	37	(d)	43	(b)	49	(b)	55	(b)
2	(b)	8	(d)	14	(d)	20	(d)	26	(b)	32	(d)	38	(b)	44	(a)	50	(b)	56	(b)
3	(d)	9	(d)	15	(a)	21	(d)	27	(b)	33	(d)	39	(b)	45	(d)	51	(d)	57	(b)
4	(a)	10	(b)	16	(c)	22	(b)	28	(a)	34	(c)	40	(b)	46	(a)	52	(c)	58	(c)
5	(a)	11	(c)	17	(d)	23	(c)	29	(d)	35	(b)	41	(b)	47	(c)	53	(d)	59	(d)
6	(c)	12	(d)	18	(b)	24	(c)	30	(d)	36	(b)	42	(c)	48	(c)	54	(d)	60	(c)

📝 Grammar

1	(a)	6	(d)	11	(b)	16	(d)	21	(a)	26	(d)	31	(c)	36	(a)	41	(c)	46	(c)
2	(b)	7	(c)	12	(b)	17	(d)	22	(c)	27	(a)	32	(b)	37	(c)	42	(b)	47	(c)
3	(b)	8	(c)	13	(a)	18	(a)	23	(b)	28	(b)	33	(b)	38	(a)	43	(b)	48	(a)
4	(b)	9	(b)	14	(c)	19	(b)	24	(c)	29	(a)	34	(d)	39	(d)	44	(b)	49	(d)
5	(a)	10	(d)	15	(a)	20	(d)	25	(b)	30	(b)	35	(b)	40	(c)	45	(d)	50	(d)

📢 Vocabulary

1	(b)	6	(d)	11	(c)	16	(d)	21	(a)	26	(a)	31	(d)	36	(a)	41	(b)	46	(d)
2	(d)	7	(a)	12	(b)	17	(d)	22	(c)	27	(d)	32	(c)	37	(a)	42	(a)	47	(a)
3	(d)	8	(b)	13	(b)	18	(a)	23	(c)	28	(b)	33	(b)	38	(a)	43	(a)	48	(d)
4	(b)	9	(b)	14	(c)	19	(d)	24	(c)	29	(a)	34	(d)	39	(c)	44	(b)	49	(c)
5	(b)	10	(c)	15	(d)	20	(c)	25	(c)	30	(b)	35	(c)	40	(b)	45	(a)	50	(c)

✒ Reading Comprehension

1	(d)	5	(a)	9	(d)	13	(d)	17	(d)	21	(d)	25	(c)	29	(c)	33	(a)	37	(c)
2	(a)	6	(c)	10	(c)	14	(b)	18	(a)	22	(d)	26	(d)	30	(c)	34	(c)	38	(c)
3	(b)	7	(b)	11	(d)	15	(b)	19	(d)	23	(c)	27	(b)	31	(d)	35	(d)	39	(c)
4	(c)	8	(b)	12	(c)	16	(a)	20	(c)	24	(b)	28	(c)	32	(a)	36	(d)	40	(b)

Actual Test 3

Answer Keys

🎧 Listening Comprehension

1	(a)	7	(d)	13	(b)	19	(a)	25	(b)	31	(b)	37	(d)	43	(d)	49	(b)	55	(a)
2	(d)	8	(d)	14	(b)	20	(c)	26	(a)	32	(c)	38	(b)	44	(a)	50	(b)	56	(d)
3	(d)	9	(a)	15	(c)	21	(d)	27	(c)	33	(a)	39	(c)	45	(c)	51	(a)	57	(a)
4	(a)	10	(a)	16	(c)	22	(c)	28	(a)	34	(d)	40	(a)	46	(a)	52	(c)	58	(d)
5	(a)	11	(d)	17	(d)	23	(b)	29	(c)	35	(b)	41	(c)	47	(c)	53	(a)	59	(d)
6	(a)	12	(a)	18	(d)	24	(b)	30	(c)	36	(b)	42	(a)	48	(c)	54	(b)	60	(b)

📝 Grammar

1	(b)	6	(b)	11	(b)	16	(d)	21	(d)	26	(c)	31	(b)	36	(a)	41	(c)	46	(c)
2	(d)	7	(d)	12	(b)	17	(c)	22	(b)	27	(a)	32	(d)	37	(b)	42	(a)	47	(c)
3	(b)	8	(a)	13	(c)	18	(a)	23	(c)	28	(a)	33	(d)	38	(d)	43	(d)	48	(b)
4	(c)	9	(b)	14	(d)	19	(c)	24	(b)	29	(d)	34	(d)	39	(a)	44	(c)	49	(c)
5	(b)	10	(d)	15	(a)	20	(a)	25	(d)	30	(a)	35	(b)	40	(b)	45	(b)	50	(d)

📢 Vocabulary

1	(b)	6	(d)	11	(b)	16	(d)	21	(a)	26	(c)	31	(a)	36	(a)	41	(c)	46	(a)
2	(b)	7	(a)	12	(c)	17	(a)	22	(c)	27	(d)	32	(c)	37	(a)	42	(c)	47	(b)
3	(d)	8	(b)	13	(c)	18	(a)	23	(b)	28	(a)	33	(b)	38	(a)	43	(d)	48	(b)
4	(b)	9	(b)	14	(a)	19	(c)	24	(a)	29	(d)	34	(a)	39	(d)	44	(a)	49	(c)
5	(b)	10	(a)	15	(d)	20	(b)	25	(c)	30	(b)	35	(c)	40	(c)	45	(a)	50	(a)

✏️ Reading Comprehension

1	(d)	5	(d)	9	(a)	13	(d)	17	(b)	21	(b)	25	(d)	29	(c)	33	(a)	37	(b)
2	(d)	6	(a)	10	(d)	14	(d)	18	(c)	22	(b)	26	(b)	30	(d)	34	(a)	38	(c)
3	(b)	7	(d)	11	(b)	15	(c)	19	(a)	23	(a)	27	(c)	31	(c)	35	(c)	39	(b)
4	(b)	8	(c)	12	(c)	16	(a)	20	(c)	24	(d)	28	(a)	32	(b)	36	(d)	40	(d)

 **TEPS** 등급표

등급	점수	영역	능력검정기준(Description)
1+급 Level 1+	901~990	전반	외국인으로서 최상급 수준의 의사소통 능력 교양 있는 원어민에 버금가는 정도로 의사소통이 가능하고 전문분야 업무에 대처할 수 있음. (Native Level of Communicative Competence)
1급 Level 1	801~900	전반	외국인으로서 거의 최상급 수준의 의사소통 능력 단기간 집중 교육을 받으면 대부분의 의사소통이 가능하고 전문분야 업무에 별 무리 없이 대처할 수 있음. (Near-Native Level of Communicative Competence)
2+급 Level 2+	701~800	전반	외국인으로서 상급 수준의 의사소통 능력 단기간 집중 교육을 받으면 일반분야 업무를 큰 어려움 없이 수행할 수 있음. (Advanced Level of Communicative Competence)
2급 Level 2	601~700	전반	외국인으로서 중상급 수준의 의사소통 능력 중장기간 집중 교육을 받으면 일반분야 업무를 큰 어려움 없이 수행할 수 있음. (High Intermediate Level of Communicative Competence)
3+급 Level 3+	501~600	전반	외국인으로서 중급 수준의 의사소통 능력 중장기간 집중 교육을 받으면 한정된 분야의 업무를 큰 어려움 없이 수행할 수 있음. (Mid Intermediate Level of Communicative Competence)
3급 Level 3	401~500	전반	외국인으로서 중하급 수준의 의사소통 능력 중장기간 집중 교육을 받으면 한정된 분야의 업무를 다소 미흡하지만 큰 지장 없이 수행할 수 있음. (Low Intermediate Level of Communicative Competence)
4+급 Level 4	201~400	전반	외국인으로서 하급 수준의 의사소통 능력 장기간의 집중 교육을 받으면 한정된 분야의 업무를 대체로 어렵게 수행할 수 있음. (Novice Level of Communicative Competence)
5+급 Level 5	10~200	전반	외국인으로서 최하급 수준의 의사소통 능력 단편적인 지식만을 갖추고 있어 의사소통이 거의 불가능함. (Near-Zero Level of Communicative Competence)

i-TEPS Review

국내 최초 통합 영어능력 평가
*i*ntegrated-TEPS

⇒ **의사소통에 필요한 듣기, 말하기, 읽기, 쓰기 능력을 통합하여 평가한다.**

듣기, 말하기, 읽기, 쓰기 능력은 서로 밀접한 관계를 가진 요소로 듣기, 읽기 능력 혹은 말하기, 쓰기 능력만을 단순히 측정해서는 정확한 영어능력을 평가하기 어렵다. *i*-TEPS는 유기적인 연관성을 지닌 이 네 가지 의사소통 능력을 통합적으로 측정하여 수험자의 영어능력을 정확하게 평가한다.

⇒ **변별력과 신뢰도가 있는 시험이다.**

i-TEPS는 국내 최고 권위의 영어능력 평가로 듣기, 읽기 분야에서 탁월한 변별력을 인정받은 TEPS와 국내 최초 CBT 방식의 영어 말하기 · 쓰기 시험인 TEPS-Speaking & Writing의 성공 노하우를 바탕으로 개발되었다. 실전 영어능력을 보다 정밀하게 측정할 수 있도록 세분화된 채점 요소를 적용하고 있으며, 출제자와 채점자를 어학 분야의 최고 전문가들로 선정하여 높은 신뢰도와 탁월한 변별력을 지니고 있다.

⇒ **실전 영어능력을 측정한다.**

간단한 대화를 할 수 있는 능력부터 도표를 보고 발표하는 분석력과 구성력까지, 접하는 상황에 따라 필요한 영어능력도 다양하다. *i*-TEPS는 유학이나 비즈니스 등 특정한 분야에서의 영어 활용 능력을 집중적으로 평가하는 타 시험과는 달리, 비즈니스 상황을 포함한 다양한 영어 사용 환경을 재현하여 실질적으로 활용 가능한 영어능력을 평가한다.

⇒ **경제성과 효율성을 갖춘 시험이다.**

i-TEPS는 타 통합 영어능력 평가시험에 비해 응시료가 저렴하다. 한 번의 시험으로 듣기, 말하기, 읽기, 쓰기 능력을 종합적으로 평가하여 각각의 영역을 별도로 평가해야 하는 타 시험과 비교해도 응시료 부담이 적다. *i*-TEPS는 최소의 시간과 비용으로 수험자의 영어능력을 정확히 측정하는 높은 효율성을 갖춘 시험이다.

i-TEPS 영역별 유형 및 설명

i-TEPS는 기존의 TEPS와 TEPS-Speaking & Writing 시험을 토대로 듣기, 말하기, 읽기, 쓰기 능력을 종합적으로 측정하는 통합형 시험으로 개발되었다. Listening, Grammar & Vocabulary, Reading, Speaking, Writing의 5개 영역에 걸쳐 약 3시간 동안 진행되며, 총 143문항, 400점 만점으로 구성되어 있다.

영역		문제유형	문항수	시간		총점
Listening	Part 1	짧은 대화를 듣고 이어질 대화로 가장 적절한 답 고르기	15	35분		80점
	Part 2	긴 대화를 듣고 질문에 가장 적절한 답 고르기	15			
	Part 3	담화를 듣고 질문에 가장 적절한 답 고르기	10			
Grammar & Vocabulary	Part 1	대화문의 빈칸에 가장 적절한 답 고르기	15	20분		20점
	Part 2	단문의 빈칸에 가장 적절한 답 고르기	15			
	Part 3	대화문의 빈칸에 가장 적절한 어휘 고르기	15			20점
	Part 4	단문의 빈칸에 가장 적절한 어휘 고르기	15			
Reading	Part 1	지문을 읽고 빈칸에 가장 적절한 답 고르기	10	40분		80점
	Part 2	지문을 읽고 질문에 가장 적절한 답 고르기 (1지문 1문항)	19			
	Part 3	지문을 읽고 질문에 가장 적절한 답 고르기 (1지문 2문항)	6			
Speaking	Part 1	간단한 질문에 대답하기	1(3)		답변 10초	100점
	Part 2	소리내어 읽기	1	준비 30초	답변 45초	
	Part 3	일상 대화 상황에서 질문에 답하기	1(5)	준비 15초	답변 10초	
	Part 4	그림 보고 연결하여 이야기하기	1	준비 60초	답변 60초	
	Part 5	도표 보고 발표하기	1	준비 120초	답변 90초	
Writing	Part 1	받아쓰기	1	10분		100점
	Part 2	이메일 쓰기	1	15분		
	Part 3	의견 쓰기	1	30분		
계						400점

TEPS

Test of English Proficiency

developed by

Seoul National University

TEPS

Test of English Proficiency
developed by
Seoul National University

청 해 Listening Comprehension

문 법 Grammar

어 휘 Vocabulary

독 해 Reading Comprehension

수험번호 Registration No.

성명 Name — 한글 / 한자

문제지번호 Test Booklet No.

주민등록번호 National ID No.

수험번호 Registration No.

비밀번호 Password

좌석번호 Seat No.

고사실번호 Room No.

감독관확인란

TEPS

Test of English Proficiency
developed by
Seoul National University

성명 | 영문
| 서명

단체 구분

학생 ○   일반 ○

질 문 란

1. 귀하의 TEPS 응시목적은?
　ⓐ 입사지원　ⓑ 인사고과
　ⓒ 개인실력측정　ⓓ 입사
　ⓔ 국가고시 지원　ⓕ 기타

2. 귀하의 영어권 체류 경험은?
　ⓐ 없다　ⓑ 6개월 미만
　ⓒ 6개월 이상 1년 미만　ⓓ 1년 이상 2년 미만
　ⓔ 2년 이상 3년 미만　ⓕ 3년 이상

3. 귀하께서 응시하고 계신 고사장에
대한 만족도는?
　ⓐ 0점　ⓑ 1점
　ⓒ 2점　ⓓ 3점
　ⓔ 4점　ⓕ 5점

4. 최근 1년내 TEPS 응시횟수는?
　ⓐ 없다　ⓑ 1회
　ⓒ 2회　ⓓ 3회
　ⓔ 4회　ⓕ 5회 이상

학력

졸업 / 재학

초등학교 | 중학교 | 고등학교 | 전문대학 | 대학교 | 대학원

전공

인문 | 사회과학·법학 | 경제학·경영학 | 자연과학 | 의학·약학·간호학 | 교육학 | 음악·미술·체육 | 기타

직업

공무원 | 교사(준비) | 교수 | 군인 | 의료인 | 자영업 | 학생 | 회사원 | 무직 | 직장인 | 기타

직종

임원 | 부장 | 차장 | 과장 | 대리 | 계장 | 사원 | 인턴 | 기타

직책

국가 | 공공 | 의료 | 전문 | 금융 | 무역 | 제조 | 건설 | 정보통신 | 서비스 | 유통 | 언론 | 교육 | 기타

성 명 (성 · 이름순으로 기재)

| | EX | H | O | N | G | | G | I | L | | D | O | N | G |

| | EX | A | B | C | D | E | F | G | H | I | J | K | L | M | N | O | P | Q | R | S | T | U | V | W | X | Y | Z |

응시일자 : 20　　년　　월　　일

〈부정행위 및 규정위반 처리규정〉

1. 모든 부정행위 및 규정위반 적발 및 이에 대한 조치는 TEPS관리위원 회의 처리규정에 따라 이루어집니다.

2. 부정행위 및 규정위반 행위는 현장 적발 뿐만 아니라 사후에도 적발될 수 있으며 모두 동일한 조치가 취해 집니다.

3. 부정행위 적발 시 당해 성적은 무효 처리되며 사안에 따라 최대 5년까지 TEPS관리위원회에서 주관하는 모든 시험의 응시자격이 제한됩니다.

4. 문제지 이외에 메모를 하는 행위와 시험 문제의 일부 또는 전부를 유출 하거나 공개하는 경우 부정행위로 처리됩니다.

5. 각 파트별 시간을 준수하지 않거나, 시험 종료 후 답안 작성을 계속할 경우 규정위반으로 처리됩니다.

[TEPS]

Test of English Proficiency
developed by
Seoul National University

수험번호 Registration No.

성명 Name
한글
한자

문제지번호 Test Booklet No.

감독관확인인

청해 Listening Comprehension

1~60

문법 Grammar

1~50

어휘 Vocabulary

1~50

독해 Reading Comprehension

1~40

주민등록번호 National ID No.

수험번호 Registration No.

비밀번호 Password

좌석번호 Seat No.

고사실번호 Room No.

서약

본인은 필기구 및 기재오류와 답안지 훼손으로 인한 책임을 지고, 부정행위 처리규정을 준수할 것을 서약합니다.

답안작성시 유의사항

1. 답안은 작성은 반드시 **컴퓨터용 싸인펜**을 사용해야 합니다.
2. 답안을 정정할 경우 수정테이프(수정액 불가)를 사용해야 합니다.
3. 본 답안지는 컴퓨터로 처리되므로 훼손해서는 안되며, 답안지 하단의 타이밍마크(▮▮▮)를 찢거나, 낙서 등으로 인한 훼손시 불이익이 발생할 수 있습니다.

4. 답안은 문항당 정답을 1개만 골라 ● 와 같이 정확히 기재하여 하며, 필기구 오류나 본인의 부주의로 잘못 표기한 경우에는 당 관리위원회의 OMR판독기의 판독결과에 따르며, 그 결과는 본인이 책임집니다.

Good ● Bad ⊘ ◖ ⊗ ✓

5. 감독관의 확인이 없는 답안지는 무효처리됩니다.

뒷면(Side2)

TEPS

Test of English Proficiency
developed by
Seoul National University

응시일자 : 20　　　년　　　월　　　일

성　명 (성·이름순으로 기재)

	EX	HONG GIL DONG
A		
B		
...		
Z		

성 명

성별 / 영어 / 서명

단체구분　학생 ○　일반 ○

질문란

1. 귀하의 TEPS 응시목적은?
   ⓐ 입사지원　ⓑ 인사정책
   ⓒ 개인실력측정　ⓓ 입시
   ⓔ 국가고시지원　ⓕ 기타

2. 귀하의 영어권 체류 경험은?
   ⓐ 없다　ⓑ 6개월 미만
   ⓒ 6개월 이상 1년 미만　ⓓ 1년 이상 2년 미만
   ⓔ 2년 이상 5년 미만　ⓕ 5년 이상

3. 귀하께서 응시하고 계신 고사장에 대한 만족도는?
   ⓐ 0점　ⓑ 1점
   ⓒ 2점　ⓓ 3점
   ⓔ 4점　ⓕ 5점

4. 최근 2년내 TEPS 응시횟수?
   ⓐ 없다　ⓑ 1회
   ⓒ 2회　ⓓ 3회
   ⓔ 4회　ⓕ 5회 이상

〈부정행위 및 규정위반 처리규정〉

1. 모든 부정행위 및 규정위반 적발 및 이에 대한 조치는 TEPS관리위원회의 처리규정에 따라 이루어집니다.

2. 부정행위 및 규정위반 행위는 현장 적발 뿐만 아니라 사후에도 적발될 수 있으며 모두 동일한 조치가 취해집니다.

3. 부정행위가 적발될 시 당해 성적은 무효 처리되며 사안에 따라 최대 5년까지 TEPS관리위원회에서 주관하는 모든 시험의 응시자격이 제한됩니다.

4. 문제지 이의에 메모를 하는 행위와 시험 문제의 일부 또는 전부를 유출하거나 공개하는 경우 부정행위로 처리됩니다.

5. 각 파트별 시간을 준수하지 않거나, 시험 종료 후 답안 작성을 계속할 경우 규정위반으로 처리됩니다.

[TEPS]

Test of English Proficiency
developed by
Seoul National University

수험번호 Registration No.
성명 Name 영글 한자

문제지번호 Test Booklet No.

감독관확인란

청해 Listening Comprehension

문법 Grammar

어휘 Vocabulary

독해 Reading Comprehension

주민등록번호 National ID No.

수험번호 Registration No.

비밀번호 Password

좌석번호 Seat No.

고사실란 Room No.

서약

본인은 필기구 및 기재오류와 답안지 훼손으로 인한 책임을 지고, 부정행위 처리규정을 준수할 것을 서약합니다.

답안작성시 유의사항

1. 답안 작성은 반드시 **컴퓨터용 싸인펜**을 사용해야 합니다.
2. 답안을 정정할 경우 **수정테이프(수정액 불가)**를 사용해야 합니다.
3. 본 답안지는 컴퓨터로 처리되므로 훼손해서는 안되며, 답안지 하단의 타이밍마크(▐▐▐)를 찢거나, 낙서 등으로 인한 훼손시 불이익을 받을 수 있습니다.

4. 답안은 문항당 정답이 1개만 골라 ① 위 같이 정확히 기재해야 하며, 필기구 오류나 본인의 부주의로 잘못 표기한 경우에는 당 관리위원회의 OMR판독기의 판독결과에 따르며, 그 결과는 본인이 책임집니다.

Good ● Bad ⊙ ① ⊗ ⦸

5. 감독관의 확인이 없는 답안지는 무효처리됩니다.

TEPS

Test of English Proficiency
developed by
Seoul National University

응시일자 : 20 년 월 일

성명	영문
평명	서명

학력

학력	재학 졸업
초등학교	
중학교	
고등학교	
전문대학교	
대학교	
대학원	

전공

인문
사회과학·법학
경제학·경영학
자연과학
어학·역학·간호학
교육학
음악·미술·체육
기타

직업

공무원
교사·준비
교수
군인
의료인
자영업
학생
회사원
주부
기타

자격

임원
부장
차장
과장
대리
주임
계장
사원
기타

직종

자영업
의료
자동차
금속기계
전기전자(관련 공학)
섬유
화학(비누·화학금융)
식음료품
유통·물류
생산관리
여행·운송
영업·유통판매
광고·홍보
부동산·건설
교육·서비스
기타
예술

단체구분

| 학생 ◯ | 일반 ◯ |

질문란

1. 귀하의 TEPS 응시목적은?
ⓐ 입사지원 ⓑ 인사정책 ⓒ 개인실력측정 ⓓ 입시 ⓔ 유학·교사 시험 ⓕ 기타

2. 귀하의 영어권 체류 경험은?
ⓐ 없다 ⓑ 6개월 미만 ⓒ 6개월 이상 1년 미만 ⓓ 1년 이상 2년 미만 ⓔ 2년 이상

3. 귀하께서 응시하고 계신 고사장에 대한 만족도는?
ⓐ 0점 ⓑ 1점 ⓒ 2점 ⓓ 3점 ⓔ 4점 ⓕ 5점

4. 최근 2년내 TEPS 응시 횟수는?
ⓐ 없다 ⓑ 1회 ⓒ 2회 ⓓ 3회 ⓔ 4회 ⓕ 5회 이상

성명 (성·이름순으로 기재)

성 EX HONG
명 GIL DONG

| | | A | B | C | D | E | F | G | H | I | J | K | L | M | N | O | P | Q | R | S | T | U | V | W | X | Y | Z |

<부정행위 및 규정위반 처리규정>

1. 모든 부정행위 및 규정위반 적발 및 이에 대한 조치는 TEPS관리위원회의 처리규정에 따라 이루어집니다.

2. 부정행위 및 규정위반 행위는 현장 적발 뿐만 아니라 사후에도 적발될 수 있으며 모두 동일한 조치가 취해집니다.

3. 부정행위 적발 시 당해 성적은 무효 처리되며 사안에 따라 최대 5년까지 TEPS관리위원회에서 주관하는 모든 시험의 응시자격이 제한됩니다.

4. 문제지 이외에 메모를 하는 행위와 시험 문제의 일부 또는 전부를 유출하거나 공개하는 경우 부정행위로 처리됩니다.

5. 각 파트별 시간을 준수하지 않거나, 시험 종료 후 답안 작성을 계속할 경우 규정위반으로 처리됩니다.

Memo

Memo

넥서스 TEPS
진품 교재 리스트

TEPS 기출문제와 전략이 있으면
TEPS 1등급 가능하다!

서울대학교 TEPS관리위원회, TEPS 전문강사, 넥서스 TEPS연구소가 탄생시킨
영역별·점수대별·전략별 TEPS 매뉴얼

TEPS 공략
No. 1 ★
기본기부터 다진다

TEPS 내실을 위한 초중급 알짜 코스
전문강사들의 노하우 공개!

How to TEPS Starter
성경준 지음 | 25,000원(MP3 CD 1장 및 부록 포함)

How to TEPS L/C·R/C
L/C 전지현 지음 | 21,500원(카세트 테이프 별매)
R/C 송영규·김정민 지음 | 19,500원

서울대 기출문제 완전 공개, 출제 유형별 적응 훈련을
위한 교재

서울대 텝스 관리위원회 제공 최신기출 시크릿
서울대학교 TEPS관리위원회 문제 제공·손진숙 해설 | 20,000원 (MP3 CD 1장 포함)

서울대 텝스 관리위원회 최신기출 1000
서울대학교 TEPS관리위원회 문제 제공·양준희 해설 | 28,000원 (MP3 CD 2장 포함)

유형별로 분석한 NEXUS TEPS 기출 800
서울대학교 TEPS관리위원회 문제 제공·문덕 해설 | 25,000원(카세트 테이프 3개 포함)

서울대 기출문제 완벽 복원
현존 TEPS 영역별 대한민국 최다 문제 수록

How to TEPS 시험 직전 리얼 시리즈
청해 넥서스 TEPS연구소 지음 | 19,500원 (Dictation Book·MP3 CD 1장 포함)
문법 장보금·써니 박 지음 | 14,000원 (TEPS 문법 핵심 비법 포함)
어휘 근간 예정
독해 근간 예정

TEPS 어휘 정복을 위한 **4주 완성 프로젝트**
난이도별로 골라서 학습하는 맞춤식 어휘집

How to TEPS VOCA 2nd Edition

김무룡 · 넥서스 TEPS연구소 지음 | 12,800원 (MP3 CD 1장 포함)

TEPS 공략
No.2 ★
전략적으로 접근한다

TEPS 초보 탈출을 위한 **기본기 형성**
청해 · 문법 · 어휘 · 독해 각 영역별 기초 지식 모음집

How to TEPS intro 시리즈

청해 강소영 · Jane Kim 지음 | 22,000원 (MP3 CD 1장 포함)
문법 넥서스 TEPS연구소 지음 | 19,000원
어휘 에릭 김 지음 | 15,000원
독해 한정림 지음 | 19,500원

TEPS 600점 이상 획득을 위한 **기초 전략 모음**
청해 · 문법 · 어휘 · 독해 각 영역별 전략 마스터키

How to TEPS 실전 600 시리즈

청해 서울대학교 TEPS관리위원회 문제 제공 · 박경숙 | 19,500원 (MP3 CD 1장 포함)
문법 서울대학교 TEPS관리위원회 문제 제공 · 이대희 | 17,500원
어휘 서울대학교 TEPS관리위원회 문제 제공 · 넥서스 TEPS연구소 | 15,000원
독해 서울대학교 TEPS관리위원회 문제 제공 · 정성수 | 19,000원

TEPS 800점 이상 획득을 위한 **마지막 통과 과정**
청해 · 문법 · 어휘 · 독해 각 영역별 고득점 지침서

How to TEPS 실전 800 시리즈

청해 강소영 · 서인석 지음 | 22,000원 (MP3 CD 1장 포함)
문법 김태희 지음 | 15,000원
어휘 넥서스 TEPS연구소 지음 | 12,800원
독해 한정림 지음 | 22,000원

● 넥서스 수준별 TEPS 맞춤 학습 프로그램

서울대 기출문제

어휘

기출·어휘
모든 점수대

기출문제집 1·2 | 서울대학교 TEPS관리위원회 문제 제공 | 272쪽 | 18,000원 (CD 2장 포함)
기출문제집 3 | 서울대학교 TEPS관리위원회 문제 제공 | 272쪽 | 19,000원 (CD 2장 포함)
NEXUS TEPS 기출 800 | 서울대학교 TEPS관리위원회 문제 제공 · 문덕 해설 | 580쪽 | 25,000원 (카세트 테이프 3개 포함)
서울대 텝스 관리위원회 최신기출 1000 | 서울대학교 TEPS관리위원회 문제 제공 · 양준희 해설 | 628쪽 | 28,000원 (MP3 CD 2장 포함)
서울대 텝스 관리위원회 제공 최신기출 시크릿 | 서울대학교 TEPS관리위원회 문제 제공 · 손진숙 해설 | 456쪽 | 20,000원 (MP3 CD 1장 포함)

How to TEPS VOCA 2nd Edition | 김무룡 · 넥서스 TEPS연구소 지음 | 320쪽 | 12,800원 (MP3 CD 1장 포함)
How to TEPS 청해 필수 표현 1000 | 유니스 정 지음 | 304쪽 | 15,000원 (MP3 CD 1장 포함)

파트별

종합서

고급
800점 이상

How to TEPS 실전 800 청해편 | 강소영 · 서인석 지음 | 436쪽 | 22,000원 (MP3 CD 1장 포함)
How to TEPS 실전 800 문법편 | 김태희 지음 | 268쪽 | 15,000원
How to TEPS 실전 800 어휘편 | 넥서스 TEPS연구소 지음 | 244쪽 | 12,800원
How to TEPS 실전 800 독해편 | 한정림 지음 | 484쪽 | 22,000원

중급
600~700점

How to TEPS 실전 600 청해편 | 서울대학교 TEPS관리위원회 문제 제공 · 박경숙 | 408쪽 | 19,500원 (MP3 CD 1장 포함)
How to TEPS 실전 600 문법편 | 서울대학교 TEPS관리위원회 문제 제공 · 이대희 | 368쪽 | 17,500원
How to TEPS 실전 600 어휘편 | 서울대학교 TEPS관리위원회 문제 제공 · 넥서스 TEPS연구소 | 384쪽 | 15,000원
How to TEPS 실전 600 독해편 | 서울대학교 TEPS관리위원회 문제 제공 · 정성수 | 380쪽 | 19,000원

How to TEPS L/C
전지현 지음 | 552쪽 | 21,500원 (카세트 테이프 7개 별매)
How to TEPS R/C
송영규 · 김정민 지음 | 592쪽 | 19,500원

초급
400~500점

How to TEPS intro 청해편 | 강소영 · Jane Kim 지음 | 444쪽 | 22,000원 (MP3 CD 1장 포함)
How to TEPS intro 문법편 | 넥서스 TEPS연구소 지음 | 424쪽 | 19,000원
How to TEPS intro 어휘편 | 에릭 김 지음 | 368쪽 | 15,000원
How to TEPS intro 독해편 | 한정림 지음 | 392쪽 | 19,500원

How to TEPS Starter | 성겸준 지음 | 564쪽 | 25,000원 (MP3 CD 1장 포함)
TEPS 첫걸음 L/C | 유니스 정 지음 | 312쪽 | 15,000원 (MP3 CD 1장 포함)
TEPS 첫걸음 R/C | 김무룡 · 넥서스 TEPS연구소 지음 | 612쪽 | 22,000원 (부록 포함)

실전
모의고사
모든 점수대

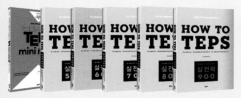

How to TEPS mini mini 1 | 서울대학교 TEPS관리위원회 편 | 164쪽 | 9,800원 (MP3 CD 1장 포함)
How to TEPS 실전력 500 · 600 · 700 · 800 · 900 | 넥서스 TEPS연구소 지음 | 308쪽 | 실전력 500~800 16,500원 (MP3 CD 1장 포함) 실전력 900 18,000원

How to TEPS 시험 직전 리얼 청해 | 넥서스 TEPS연구소 지음 | 296쪽 | 19,500원 (MP3 CD 1장 · Dictation Book 포함)
How to TEPS 시험 직전 리얼 문법 | 장보금 · 써니 박 지음 | 260쪽 | 14,000원 (TEPS 문법 핵심 비법 포함)

HOW TO
TEPS
실전력 Level 1

**취업, 승진, 진학, 고시 등 영어시험 기준 점수 획득을 위한
최고의 실전 모의고사**

18740

9 788957 974179
ISBN 978-89-5797-417-9
ISBN 978-89-5797-416-2 (SET)

값 11,000원 (MP3 CD 1장 포함)
본책의 해설집은 넥서스 홈페이지(www.nexusbook.com)에서 PDF 형태로 구입할 수 있습니다.

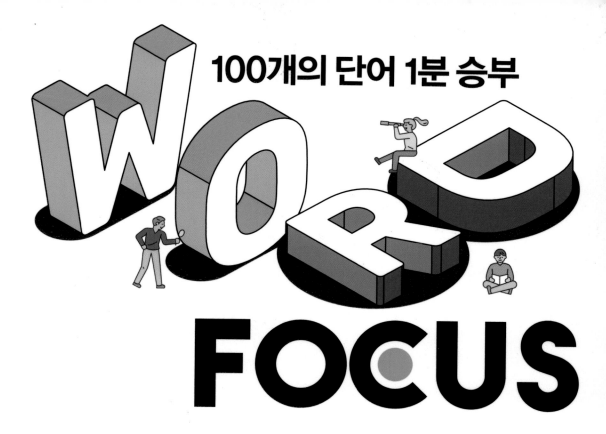

100개의 단어 1분 승부

WORD FOCUS

반요한 지음

고등 필수 명사 5000

술술 읽으면 술술 암기되는 대한민국 어휘 끝판왕

● 최단 시간에 끝내는 고등 필수 명사 어휘집
● 영어 표제어 대신 우리말 표제어로 배우는 과학적 암기 방식
● 예문 없이, 보는 순간 바로 암기되는 획기적인 구성

MP3 듣기
VOCA TEST

추가 제공 자료 www.nexusEDU.kr

원어민 발음
MP3

모바일
VOCA TEST

어휘
테스트지

NEXUS Edu

추천합니다!

모든 외국어 정복의 종착역은 결국 단어 정복이라고 말할 수 있습니다. 그러나 기존의 영단어 책들은 단순히 많은 단어들을 뒤섞어 쭉 나열하는 방식이어서 큰 효과를 거두기 어려웠습니다. 그런데 이 영단어 책은 뇌과학의 원리를 적용해 편집된 책으로 과학적이고 체계적으로 구성되어 있으며, 그냥 쭉 읽어내려가기만 해도 영단어가 자동으로 암기됩니다.

저는 영어 교육 전문가로서 이 책이 이번에 넥서스에서 정식 출판이 되기 전인 지난 1년간 이 영단어 책을 임시 제본한 책으로 제 주변의 영어 학습자들과 예전의 제자들에 이르기까지 수십 명에게 이 책의 영단어를 암기시켜 본 결과, 가장 짧은 시간 안에 즉시 외워지고 오랫동안 기억에 남는 놀라운 경험을 공유한 바 있습니다.

이 영단어 책은 여러분이 영단어 암기의 끝장을 확실히 볼 수 있도록 도와주는 대한민국 유일무이의 교재가 될 것이므로 이 책을 강력히 추천합니다.

전 이스톰 영어학원 원장, 영어교재 저술가
이준호

제가 이 책을 꼼꼼히 읽어본 결과 반 선생님은 초보 영어학습자들에게 영단어 학습의 어려움을 해결할 수 있는 새로운 길을 제시하고 있습니다. 기존 단어 책의 천편일률적인 구성을 벗어나서 학습자가 가장 쉽고 효율적으로 영단어를 기억하고 활용할 수 있도록 매우 정교하고 체계적으로 만들었음을 알 수 있었습니다.

영단어를 공부하는 데 있어서 누구나 힘들어하는 필수적인 기본 영단어 학습의 문제는 이 책을 통해 말끔히 해결될 것입니다. 영단어를 정복하고자 하는 모든 고등학생과 초보 영어 학습자에게 강력히 추천합니다.

여수 도원초등학교 교사
명태홍

이 책은 분야별로 굉장히 과학적이고 체계적으로 세심하게 편집되어 있어서 이제 영어를 제대로 배우기 시작하는 고등학생들과 그간 영어 공부를 접었다가 새롭게 영어를 배우기 시작하는 사람이라면 누구나 꼭 가지고 공부해야만 하는 필수 단어장이라고 생각합니다. 제가 이 책을 처음 보았을 때 "만약 내가 고등학생일 때 이렇게 좋은 단어책이 있었다면 얼마나 쉽고 재미있게 영어 공부를 할 수 있었을까?"라는 생각이 절로 들더군요. 영단어를 정말 쉽게 암기할 수 있는 이 놀라운 기회를 절대 놓치지 마시기 바랍니다!

영어강사
이주선